A PANAMA FOREST AND SHORE

Natural History and Amerindian Culture
in
Bocas del Toro

Burton L. Gordon

Department of Geography
and Human Environmental Studies
San Francisco State University

THE BOXWOOD PRESS

PACIFIC GROVE, CALIFORNIA

Distributed by:

The Boxwood Press
183 Ocean View Blvd.
Pacific Grove, CA 93950
U.S.A
Phone: 408—375-9110

Library of Congress Cataloging in Publication Data:

Gordon, Burton LeRoy, 1920—
A Panama forest and shore.

Bibliography; p.
Includes index.
1. Guaymí Indians—Economic conditions.
2. Natural history—Panama—Bocas del Toro (Province).
3. Rain forest ecology—Panama—Bocas del Toro (Province).
4. Indians of Central America—Panama—Bocas del Toro (Panama: Province)—Economic conditions.

I. Title

F1565.2.G8G67 1982 333.95'097287'12 82—14783

ISBN: 0-910286-88-4

Printed in U.S.A.

PREFACE

ALTHOUGH the dire ecological consequences of deforestation in the tropics are now widely recognized, efforts to slow this devastation are in disorder. Forests which once seemed protected by their sheer humid bulk are now being destroyed on a grand scale. During the last few decades the conversion of rainforests to grasslands for use in the cattle industry has been greatly accelerated. In the past such man-made grasslands were confined mainly to areas with a distinct dry season, but this is no longer the case. For example, in Bocas del Toro Province in western Panama the cattle industry is spreading despite year-round rainfall and a predominantly rough terrain. Few alternative systems of land use have been proposed. No doubt a program for protecting forests in tropical America will have to proceed on a site-by-site basis because social and ecological conditions vary. Bocas del Toro is discussed here as one such regional example. It may also serve to illustrate principles applicable to rainforest areas as a whole.

My interest in western Panama was first stimulated by the late Professor Carl O. Sauer, and by a trip there in 1953. Attracted by the area's complex natural history and hospitable people, I have since made seven field trips to Bocas del Toro—most recently in 1979. These visits lasted only one to three months each, but, distributed over so long a period, they make it possible to see historical trends which are, I think, significant for ecological planning. These observations are summarized in the following study.

I am indebted to Dr. Thomas B. Croat, Dr. John D. Dwyer, Dr. Alwyn H. Gentry, and, especially, Ronald Liesner of the Missouri Botanical Garden, St. Louis, for identifying flowering plants collected in Panama. Dr. Isabella A. Abbott and Dr. Judith E. Hansen of Hopkins Marine Station, Pacific Grove, kindly identified several marine algae. Dr. Paul H. Arnaud, Jr., Tomio Iwamoto, Michel Perekrestenko, John Simmons, and Dr. Barry Roth of the California Academy of Sciences, San Francisco, identified most of the animals collected. Marlene Dulay redrew and improved my maps.

Dr. Ralph Buchsbaum generously contributed a number of photographs, taken during his own research in Panama. Thanks are due Mildred Buchsbaum for editorial suggestions, and my wife Myra for help with typing and for all manner of encouragement. The repeated assistance of Xenia Peck, of Bocas del Toro, and Bernardo Farquez, Henry Archibald, and Orion Robinson of Río Chiriquí greatly facilitated my field work. Members of the Guaymí and Térraba tribes who have befriended and informed me over the years are too numerous to name here; this volume is a token of my appreciation.

Burton L. Gordon

Santa Cruz, California
July, 1982

CONTENTS

1

INTRODUCTION

IN PRE-COLUMBIAN tropical America tribal differences in settlement-pattern and land use gave rise to a mosaic of culturally differentiated landscapes—a productive mosaic in terms of meeting human needs, yet one in which wildlife and its habitats existed in great variety. Human settlement had spread almost throughout the rainforests.

Now, after some five centuries of European presence, rainforest vegetation has been completely eliminated over broad areas, wildlife is greatly depleted, and the aboriginal complex of forest cultures has been reduced to a few relics—exemplified here by the Indians of Bocas del Toro Province in western Panama. Native systems of land use have been replaced nowadays by commercial forms of agriculture—particularly by the banana industry and by cattle growing, a practice introduced by Europeans. Thus, the problem of habitat impoverishment and local extinction of plant and animal species is linked historically here, as in certain other areas, to the problem of disappearing human societies.

The economy of Bocas del Toro Province is predominantly biotechnic. This has been true throughout its history. Except for a brief period of Spanish gold mining, the commercial history of the Province is told in terms of its biological products—the gathered products of forest and shore and, especially, the tropical products of agriculture: sarsaparilla and chicle; coconuts and tortoise shell; cacao, rice and bananas, to name but a few. The human environment is intensely organic. Even the seasons are strongly biorhythmic in that they are sensed more obviously in the periodic reappearance of certain flowers and fruits, and in changing animal populations, than in the elements of weather. The typical problems of human subsistence involve organic interrelationships—banana diseases, leaf-cutter ants, and the tropical diseases of man. Thus the Province is discussed here mainly in terms of its plants and animals, and their uses by different peoples who have occupied the area—particularly Indian peoples.

My principal intent has been to show the ecological conditions of Indian subsistence. I have also attempted a partial description of the material culture of the Guaymí and their Indian neighbors as it relates to organic resources. Traits which link these Panamanian tribes with native cultures outside the area, especially with the Maya northward and the Zenú of Colombia, southward, have been noted—the purpose of such comparison being to show that Indian land-use practices in Bocas del Toro Province are but part of a larger complex of cultural traits once shared by many forest-dwellers to the west and south of the Caribbean.

The subsistence economy of Indian inhabitants of the area is based upon a variety of plants (foodstuff, textile and dye plants, etc.) not known in other parts of the Province. With a large selection of cultivated plants, supplemented by useful plants and animals from the forest—and especially from regrowth sites—the Guaymí make use of the varied environmental conditions found in rough terrain.

Throughout most of the Province the forest has been subjected repeatedly to a traditional Indian system of land use—a system too comprehensive to be described simply as agricultural. Under this system, agriculture is but one phase in a long-term land-use cycle which also incorporates arboriculture and the nurture of wildlife.

The stages in the cycle are marked by conspicuous changes in plant cover; and in all stages the total yield of useful products is greater than under purely natural conditions. The cycling begins with undisturbed forest, either as it existed in prehistoric times or as it may exist now in a few relatively inaccessible areas. Roughly the stages are as follows:

As a matter of Indian custom there is a constant culling of plants judged "useless" along trails and near homesites. This process of selective destruction results in a subtle reapportionment of species within parts of the forest.

During the forest clearing which precedes actual agricultural use of the soil, various valuable wild trees are left standing. Crops are then planted among these trees and almost immediately culture and harvest of several useful weedy herbs begins.

An assemblage of fruit trees in various stages of domestication (most of them not strictly native to this part of tropical America) is introduced into the clearings. And from time to time additional wild species are transplanted there from surrounding forests. Thus, orchard-like groves, now sometimes called "tree gardens," are established.

After a few years, soil depletion beneath crop plants forces abandonment or reduced use of parts of the clearings. This initiates development of a regrowth vegetation (*rastrojo*) under which the supply of soil nutrients is gradually renewed. Such regrowth proceeds through an ecological successional sequence (predominantly herbs → shrubs → trees and lianas) until forest cover is eventually reestablished. Throughout this fallow period the regrowth sites remain highly productive of food and other materials.

Such changes in habitat have potent and predictable effects upon the kinds and abundance of animal wildlife present—and thus determine the availability of those species which are commonly used as human food. Reciprocal relationships develop between plant cover and animals, with certain species (particularly those animals which disperse seeds) becoming an essential factor in carrying the land-use cycle forward.

Peoples of contrasting cultures have modified the natural setting and affected the biota differently. People of African origin in this area have a decided preference for town life, and Latin settlers stay close to roadways and the coast. Indians are the only inhabitants who take to the more isolated life in the forest, and are the only successful occupants of the rougher land away from shoreline.

No other system of human occupancy so well preserves the natural rainforest diversity.

A decrease in productive area in the Province came about in historical times with the disruption of Indian groups skilled in the arboricultural and agricultural use of this environment. In the present century a few restricted lowland sites in Bocas del Toro Province have been made very productive under commercial agriculture, especially banana growing as practiced by the United Fruit Company through its Chiriquí Land Company subsidiary. Here, towns have grown. The larger part of the Province is less productive, however, than it was at the beginning of the historical period. Historical documents and the distribution of archaeological materials indicate that areas which were formerly settled are now largely unoccupied. The same sources indicate that, despite partial depopulation as Indian contacts with Europeans increased, and despite the recent growth of urban centers, the total number of people in the Province was nearly as great in the 18th century as in the mid-20th century.

The following pages sketch these historical changes and some of the ecological and cultural circumstances under which the earlier, and more effective land use occurred and could, perhaps, be revived.

A table of terms, vernacular and scientific, arranged alphabetically, appears at the end of the text. Although the Guaymí language actually has a far more comprehensive vocabulary for the local natural history than does either English or Spanish, within the text itself common names for plants and animals from the two latter languages are used, if available, because they are more generally known. Where English terms are lacking, Spanish terms are used and written in *italics*. And where neither English nor Spanish terms exist, Guaymí terms are used instead and printed in **bold-face** type. (Of the Indian languages, Guaymí was chosen instead of Bókata or Térraba because of its larger number of speakers.) In the Guaymí language the vowels are pronounced as in Spanish, except where they carry English diacritical notations; *sh* and *aw* are pronounced as in the English words *shall* and *law*.

2

TERRAIN, CLIMATE, AND PLANT COVER

TERRAIN

Chiriquí Volcano and the Serranía de Tabasará

MOUNTAIN RANGES extend almost the length of Panama, their crests dividing the Isthmus into a series of Atlantic- and Pacific-facing slopes. Between the two principal ranges, the Serranía de Tabasará in the west and the Serranía de San Blas in the east, lies a depression—the site of the interoceanic canal—which divides Panama again, into western and eastern halves.

The Pacific, western division, commonly known as "El Interior," is commercially the most important of the four quadrants and, excluding the neighborhood of the canal itself, is the most densely settled part of the Republic. The Pan-American highway runs its length from Panamá City to Davíd, and on across the border into Costa Rica. The division facing the Atlantic is less populous and less well-known. The province of Bocas del Toro, home of the Guaymí Indians and subject of this discussion, includes the larger part of this northern division of Panama.

The extinct volcano of Chiriquí in western Panama rises to a little over 3330 m above sea level. Extending eastward from the volcano is the Serranía de Tabasará, its crest averaging some 1500 m to 1800 m above the sea. Although its surface is made up mainly of crystalline rocks, several peaks are volcanic, the highest being Cerro Santiago which rises to an elevation of about 2800 m.

Soils derived from volcanic ash are among the most fertile to be found in Panama. Such soils are extensive only on the Pacific slopes, particularly on Chiriquí Volcano. The only sizeable area of volcanic ash in the Serranía de Tabasará is on Cerro Santiago. The volcanos of the *serranía* became extinct earlier than the Volcán de Chiriquí, hence their soils are older and generally poorer. Probably the Cerro Santiago is the only peak in the range which is of Pleistocene age or later (Terry, 1956, p. 9). Volcanic ash originally deposited on the Atlantic slopes in Bocas del Toro Province has been largely eroded. Some of it has been redeposited in the alluvium of the coastal plains. (Between the upper San Pedro and Chiriquí Rivers there is a large fumarole and small lake in a crater-like depression; the steam and hot gases constantly emitted defoliate the vegetation of nearby slopes).

Almirante Bay and Chiriquí Lagoon

HUMAN POPULATION and cultural activities in Bocas del Toro Province have long been concentrated in the neighborhood of a large two-part embayment which interrupts an otherwise relatively smooth coastline. Almirante Bay is the western part of this embayment. The eastern part, deeper and less well protected from the sea, is known as Chiriquí Lagoon. (Hereabouts, people call Chiriquí Province southward on the Pacific slope "Chiriquí Afuera," i.e., "outer Chiriquí," to distinguish it from Chiriquí Lagoon and other places named Chiriquí along this Atlantic coast.) The Bay and the Lagoon are separated by Isla Popa, Cayo de Agua, and an eastward-extending peninsula of the mainland, with Split Hill near its seaward end. Isla Popa, Isla Bastimentos, Isla Colón, and Isla Cristóbal are several large islands in and around Almirante Bay, and there are hundreds of small ones. The entire embayment is roughly the size of California's San Francisco Bay.

Forest-covered ridges, roughly paralleling the Serranía de Tabasará, form the west side of Almirante Bay and rise immediately behind the shoreline. There is almost no beach within the Bay; mangrove girdles much of it and covers the lower parts of the islands. Only to the northwest of the bay is there extensive coastal lowland. There, a broad surface of alluvium, deposited by the Ríos Changuinola and Sixaola, extends from Bocas del Drago to beyond the Costa Rican border. On the other hand, there is much coastal plain around Chiriquí Lagoon; the largest area, mostly alluvial, is near the mouth of the Río Cricamola.

The Río Changuinola reaches the coast to the west of the embayment. No large streams enter Almirante Bay, West River being only a creek. The Río Cricamola, which runs northward into Chiriquí Lagoon, is the largest river entering the embayment; the Río Guarumo to the west, although much smaller, is next largest. Entering the Río Cricamola by boat is made difficult by a pronounced sandbar near its mouth. A broad beach, the only sizeable one in the Lagoon, extends away from the river mouth on either side, and sandy shallows extend well offshore.

The east side of Chiriquí Lagoon is formed by the long, northwestward-extending Valiente Peninsula. East of the peninsula and some 17 km offshore is the island, Escudo de Veraguas. Wave action is strong, and marine erosion rapid outside the embayment—except where coral reefs protect the coast. Offshore stacks appear on the seaward side of Isla Colón (e.g., at Swan's Cay), Bastimentos Island, and especially at the end of Valiente Peninsula. (Such stacks are a refuge for the brown booby; large nesting colonies are found at Swan's Cay and on Escudo de Veraguas; smaller colonies survive on Toro Cay and Tiger Rock off Valiente Peninsula near Bluefields Bay).

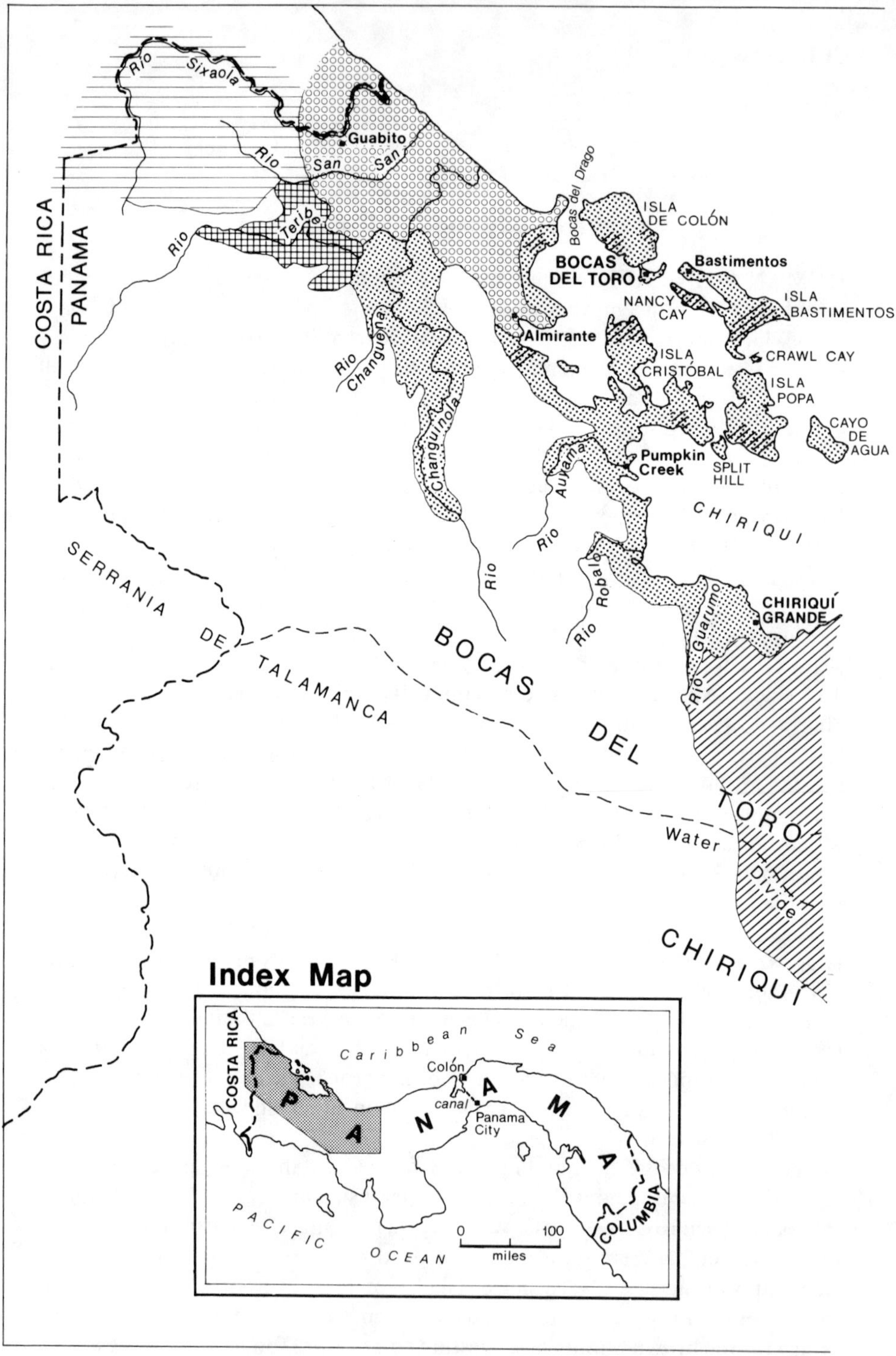
COSTA RICA
PANAMA
Rio Sixaola
Guabito
Rio San San
Rio Teribe
Bocas del Drago
ISLA DE COLÓN
BOCAS DEL TORO
Bastimentos
NANCY CAY
ISLA BASTIMENTOS
Almirante
CRAWL CAY
ISLA CRISTÓBAL
ISLA POPA
CAYO DE AGUA
Rio Changuena
Changuinola
Auyama
Pumpkin Creek
SPLIT HILL
CHIRIQUI
Rio
Rio
Rio Robalo
Rio Guarumo
CHIRIQUÍ GRANDE
SERRANIA DE TALAMANCA
BOCAS DEL TORO
Water Divide
CHIRIQUÍ
Index Map
COSTA RICA
Caribbean Sea
Colón
canal
Panama City
P A N A M A
COLUMBIA
PACIFIC OCEAN
0 100
miles

PEOPLES OF THE BOCAS DEL TORO AREA

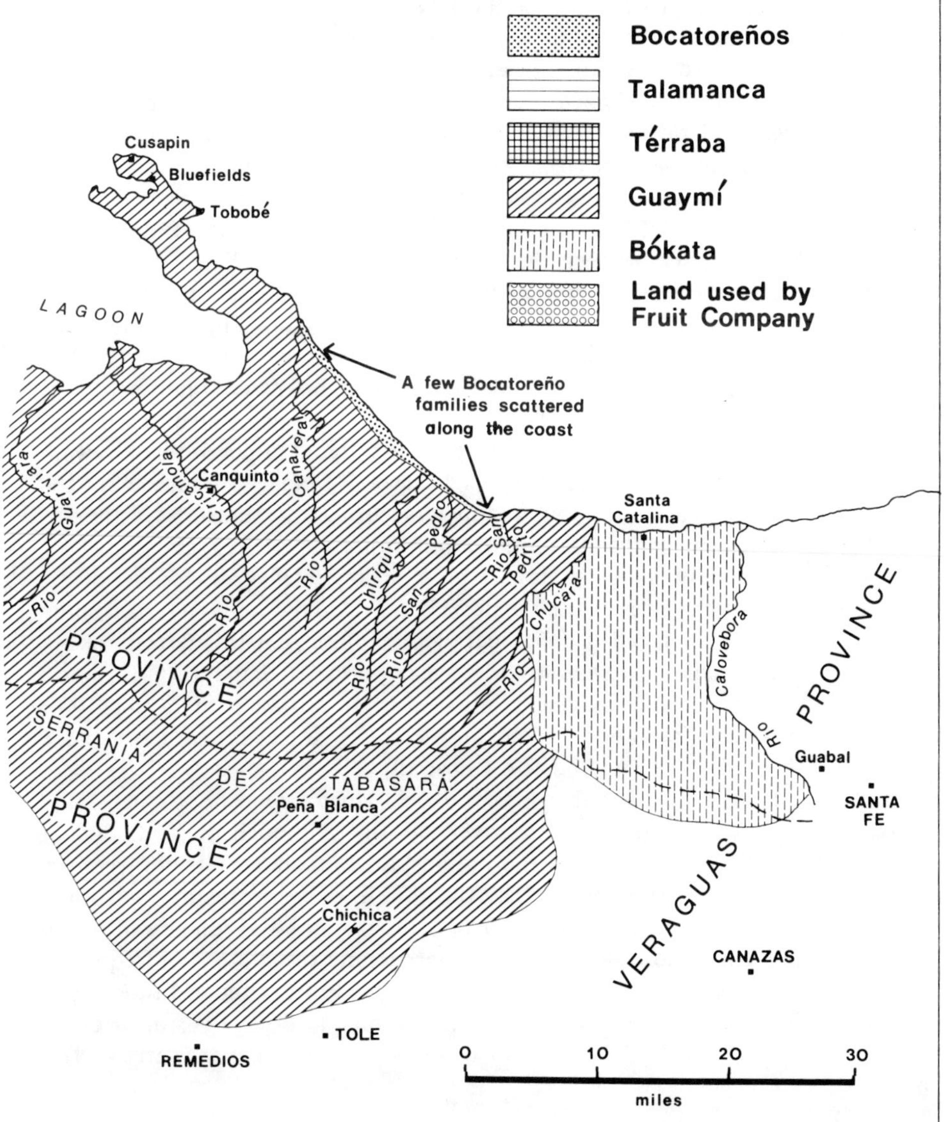

Bocatoreños
Talamanca
Térraba
Guaymí
Bókata
Land used by Fruit Company
Cusapin
Bluefields
Tobobé
LAGOON
A few Bocatoreño families scattered along the coast
Rio Guarivara
Rio Cricamola
Canquinto
Rio Canavera
Rio Chiriqui
Rio San Pedro
Rio San Pedrito
Rio Chucara
Santa Catalina
Rio Calovebora
PROVINCE
SERRANIA DE TABASARA
PROVINCE
Peña Blanca
Chichica
Guabal
SANTA FE
VERAGUAS PROVINCE
CANAZAS
TOLE
REMEDIOS
0
10
20
30
miles

The Coast from Punta Valiente to the Río Calovébora

THE VALIENTE PENINSULA is separated from coastal spurs of the Serranía de Tabasará by a broad, swampy lowland at its base which is drained by the Río Caña. The Peninsula rises to hills and offshore stacks near its tip. The rougher land is heavily forested, except for a few hills facing the coast which the Guaymí Indians have cleared in an attempt at cattle raising.

Eastward from Río Caña sharp crested ridges parallel the coast or meet it at slight angles. These ridges become higher inland, the main water divide being the crest of the Serranía de Tabasará. The crests of the higher ridges form a broken irregular skyline viewed from the Caribbean, but smaller ridges near the coast are also sharp and steep. Between the Río San Pedrito and the Río Catalina (the latter is the boundary between the Guaymí and Bókata Indians) these ridges often extend to shoreline itself and there is little low-lying coastland.

Although an almost continuous beach extends from Shark Hole, near Tobobe, eastward to Colón, in only a few spots is it as much as 45 m wide, and its width changes but little, since the tidal range is slight. Where bluff erosion is taking place, the beach is covered with shingle, in places made up of fossil coral washed out of the cliffs. The beach sand itself is soft and rather difficult to walk over, and there are many streams to cross. In several stretches one must climb the bluff and follow a path a few hundred meters through the forest. Nevertheless, the beach was probably the most important footpath on the Atlantic side of the Isthmus aboriginally, as it is today. A beach also stretches along most of the southern and eastern sides of Escudo de Veraguas. On the mainland coast many narrow linear lagoons, called *caños,* parallel the shore—separated from the sea by old barrier beaches. These *caños,* too, are important Indian transport routes: if one chooses not to walk the beach, or has much to carry, he can travel parts of this coastal stretch by canoe instead, in the *caños;* for example, most of the distance between Río Caña and Río Chiriquí.

Wave action is reduced by fringing coral reefs which extend along much of the coast, except where interrupted by river mouths. Although the reefs do not hinder alongshore movement of the Indians' dugout canoes in calm weather, they are a hazard to larger boats. Near the mouths of large streams, such as the Chiriquí and San Pedro, sand bars cause breakers and ground swell which similarly prevent motor launches from approaching the shore, and frequently even keep canoes used as tenders from going out to meet them. In the forest behind this relatively inaccessible stretch, Guaymí and Bókata custom are well preserved. Thus much of the data for this study comes from that area.

Climate

CLIMATE IS MARKEDLY different on the Atlantic and Pacific sides of Panama, especially in the amount and seasonal distribution of rainfall; average annual rainfall is much greater on the Atlantic side. The mean annual rainfall at the town of Bocas del Toro is about 287 cm and on the southeast side of Chiriquí Lagoon, somewhat higher; whereas at comparable elevations on the Pacific slope, most stations average about half that amount (Portig, 1965). There are few weather records for Bocas del Toro Province excepting those from several stations in the extreme west, but eastward the climate appears to be at least as wet.

Winter months are commonly described as the dry months in western Panama but this description, based upon records from Chiriquí Province, applies to the Pacific slope only. There, a pronounced dry season lasts from January to April. March is usually the driest month and the Chiriquí landscape is often parched then, with dusty roads and brush fires. May and November are the months of heaviest rainfall.

Although there are two periods of reduced rainfall at the town of Bocas del Toro, one in March and one in October, there is no clearly marked dry season. The mean rainfall for each of these two months is about 14 cm. There are also two periods of heavy rainfall, one usually in July and another in December or January. The average rainfall in each of these three months is about 35.5 cm. But these are averages, and monthly rainfall distribution varies so greatly from year to year that local residents recognize no persistent seasonal pattern. People here do not speak of a "dry season" or a "wet season."

Not only is the rainfall on the Atlantic side distributed more evenly over the months than on the Pacific side, but it is more evenly distributed diurnally as well. Whereas only about one-quarter of the rainfall on the Pacific side falls at night, on the Atlantic coast nearly one-half does (Cornthwaite, 1919, pp. 299-301); and this helps, also, to create nearly perpetually humid conditions there.

Plant Cover: The Rainforest and Its Marginal Vegetation

MOST OF THE province is covered by rainforest, typically a dense growth of large, predominantly broadleafed, evergreen trees. As a vegetation type, such rainforest is almost unrivalled in biotic variety and ecological complexity—the numerous species generally growing in dispersed intermixture rather than in clusters of one kind.

Although the majority of flowering plants have a seasonal reproductive rhythm, no major part of the forest vegetation fruits synchronously in any one month or two.

Evergreens greatly predominate. The few deciduous species include the hog plum and *kurutú* which shed most of their leaves in January and the *pera* which becomes completely leafless in May, at which time it blooms. Buttressed trunks are common, as on some trees of the genera *Ficus, Bombacopsis,* and *Couratari.*

Although under natural conditions the dominant trees tend to grow evenly intermixed over broad areas, in places their population densities reflect edaphic circumstances such as drainage. For example, tropical cedar is more abundant on well-drained soils than elsewhere, while the wild cashew and sandbox are most frequently seen on river floodplains. Although forest palms here rarely grow clustered together, in lowland freshwater swamps the raphia palm forms dense and extensive groves.

Comments made here are based upon observations made throughout much of the Province. But extensive collections were made only in its eastern portions, particularly on the Ríos San Pedro, San Pedrito and Chiriquí. Although the general appearance of the forest is similar throughout the Province, its floristic content varies considerably from place to place.

Brazilian tropical rainforest. Note vertical layering. As in Central America, great tracts of such forest are being leveled. (R. Buchsbaum)

Buttressed trunk of one of the rain forest giants, *Bombacopsis.* (R. Buchsbaum)

The following are among the more common, or locally best-known, large forest trees:

almendro	*Dipteryx panamensis*	Leguminosae
bateo	*Carapa sp.*	Meliaceae
breadnut	*Brosimum alicastrum*	Moraceae
cabbage bark	*Andira inermis*	Leguminosae
candlewood (*caraña*)	*Trattinnickia aspera*	Burseraceae
chutra	*Protium panamensis*	Burseraceae
johncrow wood (*yamerí*)	*Vochysia ferruginea*	Vochysiaceae
jabona	*Lacunaria panamensis*	Quiinaceae
kená	*Hirtella racemosa*	Chrysobalanaceae
kurutú	*Parkia sp.*	Leguminosae
laurél	*Cordia alliodora*	Boraginaceae
milk tree	*Conma macrocarpa*	Apocynaceae
monkey pot (*roble*)	*Couratari panamensis*	Lecythidaceae
raska	*Licania hypoleuca*	Chrysobalanaceae
sándi	*Pseudolmedia spuria*	Moraceae
sandbox	*Hura crepitans*	Euphorbiaceae
sapodilly (*níspero*)	*Manilkara bidentata*	Sapotaceae
tropical cedar	*Cedrela* sp.	Meliaceae
wild figs	*Ficus*	Moraceae
wild cashew (*espavé*)	*Anacardium excelsum*	Anacardiaceae
yellow mombin (*jobo*)	*Spondias mombin*	Anacardiaceae

Strangler fig seeds sprout high up in the tree, send their roots downward, gradually enveloping its trunk, and enter the soil. After some years, the host tree dies and decays, leaving the strangler fig as a self-supporting tree. (R. Buchsbaum)

On level land the larger trees rise to a nearly uniform height, and as their crowns form a thick shading canopy undergrowth is scattered. But most of this country is hilly or mountainous: on these slopes, where tree crowns are staggered at different levels, sunlight filters through to stimulate an undergrowth, mainly of palms and shrubs. In many places the upper canopy rising high above such undergrowth produces a roughly two-storied effect.

Although fan-leaved palms appear in the strongly seasonal climates of the Pacific slope, feather-leaved palms are characteristic in this rainforest. The briar-like sarsaparilla, also undergrowth in the forest, was long a commercial item in western parts of the Province, but it is rarely gathered now.

Flowers appear mainly in the upper canopy of the forest, and shaded surroundings near ground level are generally somber—with but a few colorful though widely-scattered exceptions. For example, almost throughout the year fluted, reddish fruits can be seen growing directly from the trunk of one small tree, *Carpotroche platyptera,* which thrives entirely in shade. And in July a medium-sized, slender tree of the mahogany family, *Guarea* sp., bears its pink flowers in short, trailing racemes which also spring directly from, and girdle, the bare lower trunk—giving a curious skirtlike effect. Most lianas bear their flowers out of sight in the branches of the trees that support them. Not so, *Schlegelia sulfurea;* in July small lavender flowers cover its leafless stem, from the ground upward. At the same time a low soft-stemmed trailing herb, the **batiya,** which grows on the steeper slopes is covered with berries and flowers, both blue; and a tiny shrub scattered over moist spots on hill country is conspicuous for its large yellow flowers. On flat land with muds rich in organic matter a leafless saprophytic herb of the gentian family, *Voyria* sp., less than 50 cm tall with a single pale stem tipped with one small lavender flower is scattered about on otherwise bare ground.

Below are listed other undergrowth plants growing in inland forest shade.

Near ground level; usually less than a meter tall:

Anthurium sp.	Araceae
Ardisia wedelii	Myrsinaceae
Besleria robusta	Gesneriaceae
Cavendishia capitulata	Ericaceae
Clidemia taurina	Melastomaceae
Drymonia pilifera	Gesneriaceae
Drymonia turrialu	Gesneriaceae
Miconia valeriana	Melastomaceae
Psychotria cooperi	Rubiaceae
Psychotria uliginosa	Rubiaceae
Renealmia chiriquina	Zingiberaceae

Growing approximately to waist height:

Aphelandra crenata	Acanthaceae
Geonoma simplicifronds	Palmaceae
Ouratea curvata	Ochnaceae
Synechanthus warscewiczianus	Palmaceae
Thecophyllum insigne	Bromeliaceae
Zamia sp.	Cycadaceae

Rising to a height of several meters:

Amphitecna latifolia	Palmaceae
Chiococca durifolia	Rubiaceae
Siparuna pauciflora	Monimiaceae

Where flooding streams have cleared paths through the forest sunshine reaches the ground, and there ribbon-like strips of light-green heliophile vegetation extend along the stream banks. Upstream, tree ferns appear occasionally on steep rocky banks. And in places the banks are completely covered by one of the most colorful shrubs of these tropics, the scarlet-leaved *Warscewiczia coccinea.* The small leguminous shrub, *Cuphea epilobifolia,* grows on sandbars, and a taller legume, *Calliandra discolor,* on rocky banks nearby.

Wild fig. *Ficus* sp. The genus includes a number of large forest trees, as well as several species with the "strangling" habit.

This cycad, **mugú,** *Zamia sp.,* has cane-like stems, and rises approximately to waist height as forest undergrowth. The cylindrical fruiting structure, which contains many red seeds, is eaten by agoutis and pacas. The pulp in the fruit's center is used by the Guaymí to stop bleeding.

Wild cane, *Gynerium sagittatum,* growing on low river floodplains. The stalks are used in many ways, e.g. for poling canoes upriver and making bird snares.

Tree ferns growing on steep rocky banks along the Río Teribe.

Downstream, heliconias and other Scitaminae are common, as is wild cane, on flat stretches with silty soil. Balsa seedlings and wild senna spring up on sandbars and cobble patches exposed along the river channels, but they are usually knocked down by floodwaters before getting more than about a meter tall. On the steeper banks stand such medium-sized trees as *Inga punctata* and *I. pezizifera,* and the following shrubs and vines (Río San Pedro and Río Chiriquí):

Allamanda cathartica	Apocynaceae
Cephaelis discolor	Rubiaceae
Cydista aequinoctalis	Bignoniaceae
Mucuna sp.	Leguminosae
Paragonia pyramidata	Bignoniaceae
Psychotria officinalis	Rubiaceae
Stigmaphyllon puberum	Malpighiaceae
Tournefortia bicolor	Boraginaceae
Warscewiczia coccinea	Rubiaceae

Closer to the Caribbean shoreline winding freshwater sloughs drain flatlands and a coastal forest, in which sapodilly, sambergum, *kurutú,* and candlewood tree are common. Beneath these on the wettest spots grow such low trees as *guagara*-palm and wild *membrillo.* A cane-like, palm *Geonoma calyptrogynoidea,* rises to a height of 3 or 4 meters. But generally plant cover beneath the forest canopy is made up of waist-high shrubs and herbs; for example, *Renealmia mexicana,* a cane-stemmed plant of the ginger family, and a madder *Cephaelis glomerulata.* Scattered among these plants are only a few low herbs; for example, a species of *Sipania* (apparently as yet undescribed), less than 30 cm tall, grows especially near slough banks. Seen characteristically on the slough bank itself are the large lavender flowers of a trailing shrub, *Paragonia pyramidata,* and red flowers of the shrub *Columnea nicaraguensis;* and, less commonly, the aroid *contra culebra.*

Fruits of the *guagara* palm, *Manicaria saccifera,* are one of the most important wild animal foods in wet lowlands, especially for peccaries. The palm's leaves are a choice roof-thatch material.

Toward the Caribbean coast the complex rainforest described above grades, on waterlogged lowland soils, into a simpler and lower forest dominated by comparatively few species—the two most common trees being sambergum and orey. Patches of such forest are found all along the coast and are extensive on the larger islands of Almirante Bay. In July, sambergum, a smooth-barked tree, produces its clusters of fragile rose-red, globular flowers in such quantity that they often redden the forest floor. With the *laurél* it is the most important lumber tree commercially logged in the area, partly because of its accessibility from the shore. The orey, which has very soft wood, has also been harvested in small amounts from time to time, for pulp.

In several lowland areas, rainforest is replaced by another, and very different, plant cover: a massive, thick-trunked feather palm (*Raphia taedigera*) forms dense, almost impenetrable groves in swamps on the lower flood plains of the larger rivers. These palm groves, known locally as *silicos,* are extensive in the lower Changuinola Valley and westward they cover even larger areas in Costa Rica (Skutch, 1946). To the east, Raphia palm groves are also found in old river meanders in the lower Cricamola Valley. (The genus *Raphia* has, incidentally, a curiously discontinuous distribution, being also found in Africa.)

Close to shoreline, rainforest gives way to a variety of coastal plant associations, of which the most extensive are the following:

1. Mangrove: Areas of mangrove-cover, known locally as *manglares,* are found in offshore shallows and extend inland from shoreline on silt deposits which are permeated with salt water. Mangrove completely covers many islets around Almirante Bay (providing roosts for numerous brown pelicans) and extensive tracts on the leeward sides of larger islands.

2. Lagoon vegetation: Water in the *caños* is brackish; and where it is especially salty the banks are fringed with mangrove. Elsewhere the banks are covered by the provision tree, beach hibiscus, wild soursop, wild calabash, and often by dense linear stands of a woody aroid (*Montrichardia*). Swamp spiderlily and *caño*-grass grow, half submerged, in shallow water near the banks.

Floodplain vegetation on the banks of the lower Cricamola River. Behind the grass-covered banks, a woody aroid (*Montrichardia arborescens*) grows to a height of about 3 m. Inland, beyond the natural levee, raphia palms cover large areas of swampy lowland.

3. Beach vegetation: Inland from the bare intertidal zone, barrier beaches are well overgrown with sea grapes, tropical almond (an introduced Asiatic tree), cocoplums, mahó, spiderlilies, etc.—or planted to coconuts.

Sea grape: flowering spike, immature fruit, and seeds — on the beach near the mouth of the Río Chiriquí; late December.

The spider lily, *Hymenocallis littoralis,* a characteristic beach plant along the Caribbean side of the Isthmus, was one of the first plants described from the New World (Oviedo y Valdés, *Historical General* ... 1535); it is now a widespread horticultural favorite.

Coco plum, *Chrysobalanus icaco,* a shrub at inland edge of beach. There are two varieties; one with red fruits, another with white. The edible plums have a cottony texture, juice is tart and astringent. Both fruits ripen in December-February, when the plants are also bearing flowers. The plant gives Coco-plum Point its name.

Wild soursop, *Annona glabra,* a medium-sized tree found on estuary banks and in nearby secondary growth. The fruit, which ripens in July, is smaller than that of the domesticated soursop, and its flesh is orange rather than white. The fruits, which have a very pleasant odor, are eaten by many animals and, occasionally, by Guaymí children.

The provision fruit tree, *Pachira aquatica,* grows in low, wet spots on the islands of Almirante Bay and Chiriquí Lagoon, and on estuary banks elsewhere along the coast. The fruit is somewhat larger than a grapefruit and contains chestnut-sized seeds which are eaten in times of food scarcity by the Guaymí and by others elsewhere in Central America. Whereas the tree flowers in July on the Pacific slope (Allen, 1956, p. 281), here its main season of flowering is between December and February.

4. Sub-tidal vegetation: Within Almirante Bay and Chiriquí Lagoon marine grasses cover broad patches of sand and silt bottom in shallow waters: turtle grass (*Thalassia* sp) with broad, ribbon-like leaves and manatee grass (*Cymodocea manatorum*?) with threadlike leaves. On the open coast these are almost lacking, being replaced by marine algae such as *Bryothamnion* on rocky shorelines and, on offshore reefs, *Sargassum* (algae of this genus are well-known for the great floating beds—the "Sargasso Sea"—which they form as they drift eastward into the Atlantic).

Sargassum, an alga, grows attached to rocks along tropical and substropical shores. Masses break loose and continue to grow, floating in the open sea, moved about by wind and currents. These masses become home for a community of animals which take on the coloration and pattern of the alga. Here is a sargassum fish, highly adapted to this community in its coloration and behavior. Its dorsal fins are modified to hold on to the alga. Other members of the community include a crab, nudibranch, bryozoans, shrimp, snail, and others—all integrated into the sargassum community. (R. Buchsbaum)

Southward, beyond the limits of this study, the tropical rainforest grades on the highest peaks of the Serranía de Tabasará into a dwarf forest or woodland of northern genera: elderberries, alders and *Escallonia* (Pittier, 1918). Passing over the crest of the *serranía* out of Bocas del Toro Province, the forest ends abruptly a short distance down the Pacific slope in an irregularly horizontal tree line, below which the land has been cleared for cattle grazing. There, the landscape is of a kind not found in Bocas del Toro Province: high and cool with steep, grass-covered hills, gorges, waterfalls and long views. Coffee is grown on the middle slopes, for instance around the town of Santa Fe. Below, in the savannas of Veraguas and Chiriquí, there is a good deal of regrowth shrub which local cattlemen, some of them Guaymí Indians, try to keep cut back.

Savannas on the Pacific side of the Serranía de Tabasará—strewn with volcanic rocks—upslope from Santa Fe, looking northward. Note the extensive clearing and pastures on the slopes and the edge of the rainforest near the crest of the Serranía de Tabasará in the background. This is at the south boundary of Bocas del Toro Province.

3

ETHNOGRAPHY: PAST AND PRESENT

URBAN POPULATION is concentrated almost entirely in the western part of the Province. Changuinola, Almirante and Bocas del Toro (generally called simply "Bocas") are the three largest towns. Changuinola is the local headquarters of the Chiriquí Land Company, as the United Fruit Company is called here. As the only large commercial enterprise, the United Fruit Company has dominated the economy of the Province for over half a century.

Although sparsely settled, Bocas del Toro Province is culturally diverse. A classification of inhabitants based upon differences in language, religion, material culture, geographical origin, and race distinguishes the following as the principal groups: the Guaymí Indians and their close cultural relatives, the Bókata; the Térraba Indians; the Bribri Indians, a sub-group of the Talamanca tribe of Costa Rica; the Cholos along the Veraguas boundary; the San Blas (Cuna) Indians, migrant laborers in the banana industry; the Bocatoreños, subdivided in local terminology into "Criollos," who are culturally Latins, and "Natives," of predominantly Anglo culture; Chiricanos, recent Panamanian immigrants from the Pacific slope of the Isthmus; and Chinese.

The Indians, taken as a group, outnumber any of the others—the Guaymí being by far the largest tribe, followed by Bókata and Térraba. After Indians the two largest groups are the "Natives" (Bocatoreños) and the Chiricanos. Today, the latter two groups are probably about equally numerous, the population of Chiricanos having greatly increased during the last twenty years.

Peoples of Bocas del Toro Province

THE FOLLOWING summary briefly describes the peoples of Bocas del Toro Province:

Guaymí Indians

THE GUAYMÍ are widely distributed in western Panama. On the Atlantic side of the isthmus the areas of densest Guaymí settlement in Bocas del Toro Province are the upper Cricamola River, the valley of the Río Caña, and the tip of Valiente Peninsula. Eastward their territory extends as far as the Río Chutra, the boundary between them and the Bókata Indians.

A considerable number of Guaymí live on the Pacific slopes of Panama in the savannas of Chiriquí and Veraguas Provinces. On the southern side of the isthmus they are found downslope well beyond the edge of the forest, raising cattle and gardening in the savannas (Young, 1971). The lower boundary of their territory roughly parallels the highway from Panamá City to Davíd, lying generally well inland from it, except near Remedios. The easternmost extent of Guaymí on the Pacific slope is in Veraguas Province.

But the Guaymí discussed on the following pages practice an older form of livelihood, with a different subsistence base—and better-preserved horticultural traditions, in the forests of Bocas del Toro Province.

The Guaymí are one of the most rapidly increasing tribal populations in the Americas. The total number is uncertain, but there are well over 40,000, of which more than one third live in Bocas del Toro Province. There is little doubt that the Guaymí form the largest Indian group in the Republic. They are a principal subject of this study, and discussed in detail below.

Bókata Indians:

THE BOKATA live in the extreme eastern part of the Province, mainly along the western tributaries of the Río Calovébora—that river being their eastern boundary. Their territory lies entirely on the Atlantic slope—that is, entirely in Bocas del Toro Province—where their houses extend almost to the crest of the Serranía de Tabasará. Their western boundary is near the Río Chucara whose resources they share with their neighbors, the Guaymí.

Bókata house on the Río Caoita. The vine growing over the roof is *Sechium edule*, the cucurbit known as *chayote* in Mexico.

Although the Bókata and Guaymí languages are related and have a number of terms in common, they are mutually unintelligible. Physically the two peoples also differ slightly, the Bókata being somewhat smaller and their men, more heavily bearded. In material culture and land use the Bókata closely resemble the Guaymí but details differ. For example, travelling Bókata can usually be distinguished from Guaymí by the manner in which they carry belongings: the Bókata use a carrying frame (an *encañizo* or *jaba,* as it is called by Panamanians around Santa Fe) or a basket, while Guaymí carry their belongings in a distinctive net carrying bag. Bókata and Guaymí housetypes also differ somewhat.

The Bókata are less influenced by outsiders than are most Guaymí. This is mainly the result of geographical isolation; Bókata territory was, until recently, the least accessible part of western Panama. Within the last few years part of an old Indian trail has been broadened into a road, and in good weather it is now possible to drive over the mountain crest to the headwaters of the Río Calovébora. (The name Bókata—although described by Nordenskiold and others as being of obscure origin—is probably simply an elided "Bocatoreño," as pronounced by Indians and Cholos of neighboring Veraguas Province, when referring collectively to the inhabitants of Bocas del Toro Province.)

Térraba Indians

NEAR THE COSTA RICAN border of the Province, a small Indian tribe inhabits the valley of the Río Teribe, the largest tributary of the Río Changuinola. These Indians, known locally as Teribes, appear in ethnographical literature under the name Térraba. In their own language, they refer to themselves as *Náso.* Although they still speak their native language, adults speak Spanish as well and have adopted Spanish personal names. The Térraba travel up and down river in dugout canoes and are frequently seen at the bridge where the Company railroad crosses the Río Changuinola, a place called Torres. A few hours upstream by canoe, across the river from the *finca* of a prosperous Bocatoreño family, is Hueksó—beyond which all inhabitants are Indian.

A Térraba family.

Cholos

LIKE THE BRIBRI INDIANS this group is located near or outside the boundaries of the Province, and thus discussed only briefly.

The term "Indian," as used hereabouts, is more a cultural than a racial term. Spanish-speaking persons of Indian physiognomy are known as "Cholos." Such is the population in parts of the Río Calovébora Valley and eastward into the Province of Veraguas—for example, at Guabál, an attractive settlement scattered around the junction of the Calovébora with its tributary, the Río Piedra.

Although the people at Guabál are Christians and consider themselves in all respects Panamanians, they have a number of aboriginal traits—some in common with the Bókata and Guaymí. For example, many men and women have their teeth filed or broken to a point. And as among the Guaymí, two hearths are occasionally seen in their houses, one for the sick. They are good craftsmen and make net hammocks and hats for trade in Santa Fe. These Cholo people may be remnants of the various more civilized Panamanian tribes which, like the Coiba and Cueva, disappeared quickly after the Conquest.

Bribri Indians

THE BRIBRI are a small branch of the large Talamanca tribe. Most, like the rest of the Talamancas, live in Costa Rica. The few on the Panamanian side of the boundary live to the south of the middle Sixaola River, mainly on its tributary, the Yorkín. The Talamancas mix more freely with outsiders than do other Indians hereabouts.

In Costa Rica a United Fruit Company railroad track runs up into the territory of the eastern Talamancas. A good many of them in that neighborhood work for the Company. Like the Térraba they have become quite dependent upon supplies brought in by the railroad. Ministers travel to their settlements from Almirante on Sundays by rail, and many have become Protestants.

Bocatoreños

THOUGH THE NAME may be applied by other Panamanians to the inhabitants of Bocas del Toro Province in general, within the Province itself the term "Bocatoreño" refers to only one large bipartite group, the major non-Indian element in the population. An old and persistent cultural cleavage divides the Bocatoreños into two subgroups, known locally as "Criollos" and "Natives"—one representing a Latin, the other an Anglo, tradition.

1. Criollos: Although most of the people called "Latins" in the Province are recent immigrants from Chiriquí Province, a number of large families have been residents since this territory was Colombian. They are predominantly descendants of early Spanish settlers with some Indian and Negro admixture (the latter from Colombian, rather than Jamaican, sources). Spanish-speaking with Spanish surnames, they are mostly Roman Catholic. Many speak no English.

The town of Bocas del Toro, capital of the province, on Isla Colón.

The Criollos are settled mainly around the northwest shores of Chiriquí Lagoon between Chiriquí Grande and Split Hill, on Isla Popa, and are scattered along the shoreline in Guaymí country eastward toward Veraguas Province. Few live in the town of Bocas itself, except those who are government employees.

The Criollos lead an amphibious existence: on Chiriquí Lagoon their pile houses, generally with corrugated iron roofs, are set out over the water along the shore. (They jest about having snakes in their backyard, sharks in the front). As with the Guaymí, their only vehicles are dugout canoes, in which they carry farm products to Almirante and Bocas, and shop at their scattered coastal stores. The Criollo is a Latin with a canoe instead of a horse—that animal being quite useless on these beachless, tropical islets. Tiny children paddle off to school. For Criollos living on Chiriquí Lagoon, going to town means going to Bocas. Even with an outboard motor this takes several hours; paddling, it may take a day and half the night. It can be a wild ride in a hollowed log. Sometimes the waters of Chiriquí Lagoon get rough; they are deeper and more exposed to the sea than are the waters in Almirante Bay. Often the entire family goes.

Close by most Criollo houses are small plaintain groves, rice fields, and patches of sugar cane. Farther back from shoreline on the rougher land are cacao orchards, a principal commercial resource. Along the beaches of the eastern part of the Province, coconuts are the major crop, and an increasing number of the more prosperous families are clearing land for cattle. In fact, Criollos are, with the Chiricanos, the bearers of Spanish tradition—under which cattle, rice, sugar cane, and bananas were carried to the New World and eventually to Bocas del Toro Province.

Bocatoreños, or simply "Toreños" as they are often called, are the principal intermediaries between the Guaymí and the towns. Many make their living mainly from trade with the Indians and, since Toreños often marry Guaymí women, some are of partly Guaymí descent and speak Guaymí.

Bocatoreño ("Criollo") dwellings near Split Hill

2. **Natives:** In Bocas del Toro Province the people called "Natives" are mainly Protestant Negroes with British family names, whose mother tongue is English. The Native population is mainly urban, though some live along the shores of Almirante Bay. Thus, the peninsula separating the Bay from Chiriquí Lagoon is occupied by Natives on the northwest aide, Criollos on the southeast. By far the greater number of inhabitants of Bocas are Negro, and the town of Old Bank on Bastimentos Island is entirely so.

These people are descendants of English-speaking immigrants from Caribbean islands. A principal source was the Colombian islands of San Andreas and Providence. Actually, the town of Bocas, founded in 1826, appears to have grown from a camp of English-speaking settlers from San Andreas, trading here in shell of the hawksbill turtle (Parsons, 1972, p. 59). Another source was Jamaica, the arrival of Jamaican laborers in Panama having been a consequence of two American ventures—the building of the interoceanic canal and, more important, the development here of the banana industry by the United Fruit Company.

Religious activities thrive among the Natives. Religion is jokingly referred to as the second biggest business in the Province—after bananas. There are a dozen or so denominations, some unorthodox; for instance, "obeah" (witchcraft) is almost as strong here as in the West Indies, and has crept into the ritual of several minor Christian sects. In this connection there is a curious social tie between the Natives and the Indians in neighboring Costa Rica: Talamanca *sukias* (witch-doctors) are the most esteemed counselors in the practice despite its largely Afro-Jamaican origins, and are often visited by Natives for advice.

The Panamanian government has been making a moderately successful effort to supplant the English language with Spanish (for instance, two decades ago signs in the plaza at Bocas read "Hable Castellano, somos Panameños." And Protestant ministers who preached in English were supposed to re-read the sermons to their congregations in Spanish, but the regulation was commonly disregarded). As Spanish is compulsory in the public schools, most young people are now bilingual. Lately an attachment to English has revived among Native residents and many are asking that English classes be established in the schools.

Urban gardens and cookery preserve the West Indian heritage. Such cultivated plants as breadfruit, jackfruit, ake, otaheite apple and sorel are among the numerous cultural contributions to the Province made by immigrants from islands of the Caribbean, though, to be sure, these plants actually originated outside the Americas.

San Blas (Cuna) Indians

CREWS OF SAN BLAS come here from their country east of Colón to work for the United Fruit Company; they live mostly in Changuinola and Almirante; only a few have brought women with them. The Company has found the San Blas to be ideal employees: temperate, close-mouthed, and hardworking. They and the Guaymí are the principal field labor force in the banana plantations. These days they try to avoid work as *macheteros* which they consider beneath their dignity; it is the Guaymí employees who chop and carry the banana bunches from the fields. Several San Blas have risen to positions of real responsibility. Not so the Guaymí, who are at the bottom of the social heap. Other Indians speak of the San Blas with respect. Although the San Blas talk in Cuna among themselves, most speak Spanish, and a good many speak English.

Chiricanos

MOST OF THESE PEOPLE came by plane from Chiriquí Province in recent years to work for the Company. They have become an important part of the work force. Many are employed as office help and foremen in the plantations. Others are finding a place elsewhere in the local economy; for instance a number have started cattle ranching to supply meat to the Company towns. There are a number of such ranches around Chiriquí Grande, at the end of the cattle trail from Chiriquí Province, and at Miramar.

Of Spanish-Indian descent, the Chiricanos speak only Spanish and are Roman Catholic. Thus, they reenforce the social influence of the Criollo element in the population. They bring to the Province the strong emphasis on cattle growing which characterizes the economy on the Pacific slopes of the Isthmus, and have introduced a number of the African forage grasses now being grown in local pastures.

Chinese

THERE ARE SEVERAL hundred Chinese in the Province. Most are of Cantonese origin and teach their children Cantonese as a first language; all speak Spanish or English. They seldom marry non-Chinese.

The Chinese here are usually in business and are quite successful; for example, there are only a few stores in the predominantly Negro town of Bocas which are not owned by Chinese. Two Chinese-owned launches ply the coast between Bocas and Colón carrying supplies and, in season, buying hawksbill turtle shell and spiny lobsters from the Guaymí.

Guaymí and Neighboring Tribes in the Past

1. **Subsistence in Pre-Columbian Times.** On the peninsula separating Chiriquí Lagoon from Almirante Bay, on nearby islands, and on inland hills west of the Lagoon prehistoric inhabitants have left behind extensive midden deposits consisting mainly of mollusk shells (Gordon, 1962). Some of the shell mounds are within a short distance of the coast, e.g., on Cerro Brujo; others, for example those located in unoccupied forest land between the Río Guarumo and Río Changuinola, are at least six kilometers from shoreline. Many of the deposits are over 50 m long and 30 m wide; depths of shell accumulation range from a few centimeters to about two meters. The shells are largely fragmented, compacted, and cemented with black, sticky soil. Few such shell deposits have been found elsewhere on the Atlantic coast between Colombia and Nicaragua. (Recently the Cerro Brujo site has been systematically excavated by Dr. Olga Linares de Sapir and her associates of the Smithsonian Institution).

The following are some of the mollusks found in the mounds:

Apple murex	*Murex pomum*
Eared ark	*Anadara notabilis*
Bloody clam	*Anadara ovalis*
Broad-ribbed chione	*Chione latilirata*
Brown crown conch	*Melongena melongena*
China cockle?	*Trachycardium egmontianum*
Prickly cockle?	*Trachycardium isocardia*
Cross-barred Venus	*Chione cancellata*
Eared ark	*Arca auriculata*
Faust tellin	*Arcopagia fausta*
Fighting stromb	*Strombus pugilis*
Great white (tiger) lucine	*Codakia orbicularis*
Jewel box	*Chama macerophylla*
Lion's paw	*Lyropecten nodosus*
Lister's Venus	*Periglypta listeri*
Pennsylvania lucine	*Lucina pensylvanica*
Magpie shell	*Cittarium pica*
Short-frond murex	*Murex brevifrons*
Spiny lima	*Lima lima*
Spiny oyster	*Spondylus americanus*
	Thais trinitatensis
Tulip shell	*Fasciolaria tulipa*
Turkey wing	*Arca zebra*
Vase shell	*Vasum muricatum*
Zigzag scallop	*Pecten ziczac*

Fish and turtle bones are also plentiful in the midden, as are the bones of peccaries and other mammals.

One of the shells noted above, the magpie shell, though it lives abundantly near the seaward edge of this embayment seems to be disappearing from other parts of its range: "It is frequently seen in old Indian shell heaps along the Florida coast ... but there are only one or two questionable records of live examples occurring there in the last decade" (Morris, 1973, p. 112).

The complete familiarity of the midden makers with the marine environment is attested to by the great variety of marine organisms present in the deposits; further evidence of their bonds with the sea is the frequent appearance of marine creatures as art motifs on potsherds.

Marine animals and other aquatic animals (fish, crab, crocodilians, etc.) on pre-Columbian pottery from Cerro Brujo. Potsherds, and other artifacts collected by the author in 1953 were donated to the Lowie Museum of Anthropology, University of California, Berkeley, which kindly provided this photograph. The figures are on very large, heavy-walled (ca. 6 cm thick) pottery, which was probably used either for water cisterns or in communal cooking.

The midden shells represent virtually the whole range of mollusk habitats in the embayment: Shallow water species include the eared ark, found especially on muddy bottoms; the bloody clam and great white lucine, on sandy bottoms; the apple murex, on gravel bottoms; the magpie shell and turkey wing on rocks; the vase shell, on coral; the short-frond murex, on mangrove roots, etc.

The frequent occurrence of some mollusks in the midden shows that diving was done regularly to remarkable depths. Listed below are usual depths for seven species (Morris, 1973):

zigzag scallop	10 to 25 m
little white lucine	10 to 25 m
faust tellin	10 to 25 m
broad-ribbed chione	25 to 60 m
jewel box	25 to 60 m
lion's paw	25 to 60 m
spiny oyster	25 to 60 m

Mingled with larger shells in the middens are many others so tiny that it is hard to believe that they yielded food enough to justify their collection and transport, or that they were picked by hand, individually. The harvesting of such quantities of young shellfish must at times have depleted the whole neighborhood.

The abundance of midden here is perhaps partly explained by the concentration of varied benthic habitats within this area: the embayment—semi-enclosed, island studded, and partly estuarine—is the largest to be found on the entire southwestern shore of the Caribbean. But factors other than a favorable physical environment are involved. Although mollusks were undoubtedly a much-used food in the area, these thick and localized middens were probably accumulated under unusual subsistence conditions. The shellmounds may actually mark old refuge areas. They are often situated on the higher slopes and along crests, where a good view over the embayment can be had by felling a few trees; sites of the larger middens appear to have been selected with this in mind.

The sites chosen by the midden-makers are not those favored by Indians today: these crests are among the poorer agricultural land, and a long walk from canoe landings and freshwater supplies. On the Valiente Peninsula, where the Guaymí have gathered mollusks for centuries, there are no such shell heaps.

Prehistorically this area appears to have been much contested, with incursions by Chibchans from South America, by Caribs from the east, and by northerners (probably including Nahuas). Similarly, in historical times it was invaded by Miskito Indians from Nicaragua. The midden makers may well have been lasting out the raids of such a period. (Mollusks are a dependable emergency food for a population forced to abandon most of its agriculture). Recent excavation indicates that one mound was accumulated within a surprisingly brief period, i.e. within twenty-five to fifty years, in the 10th century A.D. (Sapir and Ranere, 1971, p. 354).

Normal food-source ratios for the area as a whole are not easily judged from these unusual and short-lived middens; important as marine resources were in pre-Columbian times, marine and other animal remains are present in disproportionate quantities.

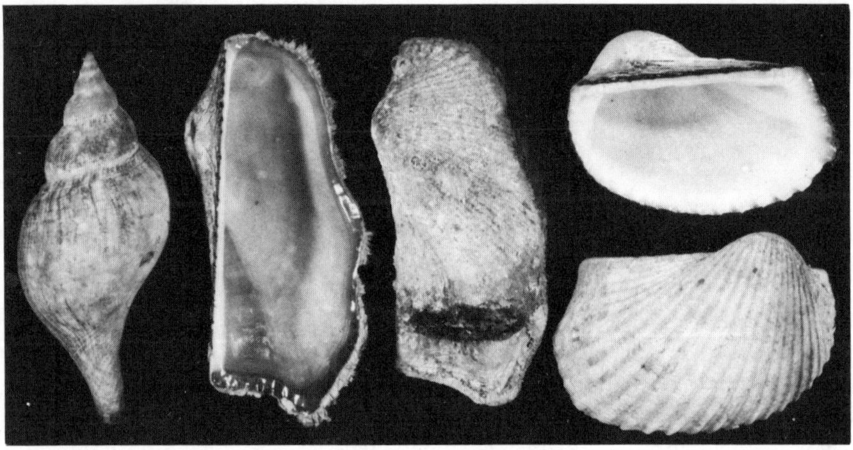

A. B. C.

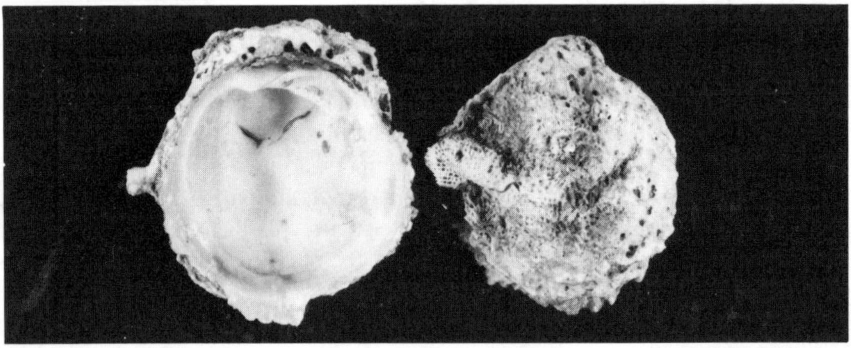

D.

A. Tulip shell; **B.** Turkey wing; **C.** Eared arc; **D.** Jewel box.

Collecting some of the mollusks found in middens here, not only required the prehistoric gatherer to dive to considerable depths, but probably to carry prying tools as well, for instance, jewel boxes are described as being "unusually firmly attached, so a hammer and chisel are necessary parts of the collector's equipment" (Morris, 1973, p. 50).

A large grinding or pounding stone (almost 1 m in length), with a slightly depressed upper surface, lying on a midden deposit west of Chiriquí Lagoon. Originally, the stone may have been used with a rocker-mano for crushing peach palm fruits, etc. (A similar tool, made of wood, is used by modern Térraba.) The stone has be re-used at some later date with a pestle as a mortar, probably for grinding maize (note the round secondary depression in its center, here partly filled with rainwater). The durable shells of the fighting stromb, seen lying nearby, often mark midden sites.

The shell collectors may not have been precursors of the Guaymí themselves, but rather of culturally related neighbors, since the shell mounds are within territory occupied in the 16th and 17th centuries by the now-extinct Dorasque, and perhaps Changuena, Indians (Léon Fernández, 1886, pp. 372 and 477).

There is some evidence indicating a parallel pre-historic change in land use among the Maya and tribes of Bocas del Toro Province—with an early land use based upon tree culture and root-crops giving way in both areas to intensive maize culture. The shell middens near Chiriquí Lagoon contain few maize-grinding stones, the implication being that at the time of their formation root-crops were the staple food here. At the surface of the midden sites, however, grinding stones are occasionally found, including a widespread Central American metate-type with four legs and a jaguar head at one end, commonly used for maize. (The latter were perhaps brought from Chiriquí Province in trade, since they are made of vesicular lava, a rock type more common there than here). By early historical times a maize was certainly being grown in Bocas del Toro Province in quantities.

During the last few years Guaymí, spreading from the southeast, have settled forest-covered parts of the shellmound area, and nearer the Lagoon Bocatoreños are clearing coastal tree growth for the expanding cattle industry.

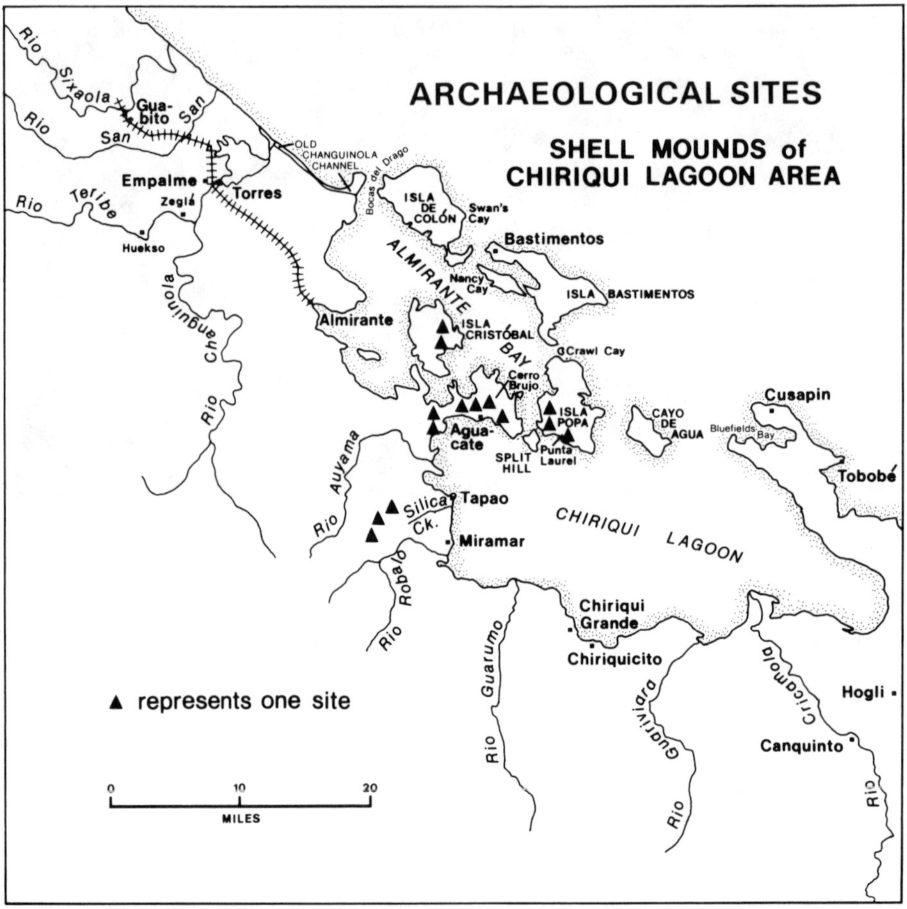

The location of a river called "Guaymí" is important in placing the various tribes of this area during the 16th to 18th centuries. The name "Guaymí" itself would lead one to look for this river on modern maps in the present territory of the Guaymí tribe, although perhaps under another name. On the other hand, while for the earliest expeditions along this coast "Valley of Guaymí" may not have been a definite locality, it soon came into frequent association with Almirante Bay, and particularly with a vicinity called Bocas del Drago at that bay's north end. In fact, the river was often described as emptying into Almirante Bay at Bocas del Drago. The following statements are from an account written in 1575: " ... it is well known that the said river of Guaymí and Bocas del Drago and Almirante Bay are one and the same thing. ..." (Léon Fernández, V, p. 84); and, in 1577, "... a river and valley called Guaymí which empty into Bocas del Drago ..." (Léon Fernández, V, p. 86).

The Río Cricamola (or Chiricamola) has been sometimes taken for the same river as the Guaymí, because it is well within the territory of the Guaymí Indians and is presently the only sizeable river which flows into the embayment. But since the Cricamola actually enters Chiriquí Lagoon rather than the Almirante Bay portion of the embayment—and

Subsistence at Conquest Time and During the Spanish Colonial Period

COLUMBUS EXPLORED this coast in 1502, on his fourth voyage to the New World, and historical records of the area are among the oldest extant for North America. Various local place names commemorate his activities here: Almirante Bay (Admiral Bay), Isla Cristóbal (Christopher Island), Isla Colón (Columbus Island). etc. Sailing from Almirante Bay to Chiriquí Lagoon, Columbus spoke of travelling "as it were in streets between one island and another, the foliage of the trees brushing the cordage of the vessels"; this may well be the narrows now called "Split Hill" (Morrison, 1942, p. 606), though there are several similar passages.

To a long stretch of land eastward from Chiriquí Lagoon (including not only a part of modern Veraguas but most of what is now Bocas del Toro Province, as well) Columbus applied the term Varagua; the term survives in Bocas del Toro Province in the name of the island Escudo de Veragua (Shield of Veragua).

When Columbus visited this part of Panama, parts of it were apparently much more open than at present; and in at least one area forests were interrupted by sizeable plantations of maize. In February 1503, the Spanish Adelantado, exploring Veragua for gold, reported that he "continued his journey with thirty men to Zobrada, *where there were more than six leagues of maize fields,* like fields of wheat." Zobrada was located in what is now either eastern Guaymí or Bókata territory. But generally the forest graded into gardens of trees and rootcrops (and, especially in late pre-Columbian times, into maize fields), interspersed with thickets of regrowth.

When the first Spanish arrived the inhabitants were reported to have "for their nourishment also much maize—from which they made white and red wine." (Sauer, 1966, p. 133). To this day the Guaymí grow a special red-seeded maize, **i-baba,** for making a fermented drink. Until as late as the seventeenth century, this was still described as an important maize-producing country and as being well peopled; numerous natives met the explorers wherever they touched shore.

---

since the Cricamola's mouth is well off to the southeast of Bocas del Drago—it is much more likely that the "Valley of Guaymí" was instead the river now called Changuinola. I think that the main stream of the Río Changuinola, which now empties largely upcoast of the embayment, entered Almirante Bay near Bocas del Toro as late as the 18th century; but the river had several mouths, or "bocas," then as now. (In the early part of the present century, when the Company had its headquarters at Bocas del Toro, a small-boat canal connected Bocas del Drago with the lower Changuinola Valley. The canal, which lies in the old channel of the Changuinola River, is now choked with water hyacinths and little used). It is taken for granted here that the river now called the "Changuinola" was once known as the "Guaymí."

In early accounts, the large islands of Almirante Bay (Isla Colón, Isla Bastimentos, etc.) near the mouths of the Changuinola were also known as the "islands of Toja" (Léon Fernández, V, p. 222). Perhaps Toja was corrupted to the Spanish "Toro," thus giving "Bocas del Toro."

Indian agriculture on the forested side of the Isthmus has changed little since it was first described. Plants cultivated by the Guaymí today are much the same as those grown in the 16th and 17th centuries, banana and rice being the only major crop plants introduced since. The peach palm, or *pejibaye,* was a staple, its fruit used for food and in making beverages—and its wood for making lances and arrows (Salcedo, 1908, p. 86). Manioc, sweet potatoes, squashes, plantains and cacao were also grown. Maize was described as being produced in abundance, and note was made at the time that in this equable climate it could be planted and harvested in any month of the year. Other products were honey and wax (from the stingless native bees), sarsaparilla, and wild pineapple fibers (Léon Fernández, 1881-1907, p. 156). In the 17th century, these Indian agriculturists were still raising tapirs and peccaries (apparently semi-domesticated here) for food and as trade items:

> There are four kinds of merchandise which they bring: tamed tapirs, peccaries, liquor, and beads. The tapirs are raised in their houses from the time they are very young. It is the custom .. for the Indian chiefs to kill these animals at their gatherings and festivals; the usual value placed on one tapir is twenty pesos, that being the value of the gold they give for it. The peccaries, which are called *zahinos,* are small and tame, and follow their masters wherever they go like dogs, even though they travel in the mountains; these also are killed at the more ordinary festivals ... four peccaries being worth one tapir (Léon Fernandez, 1881-1907, p. 156).

An aromatic liquor, resembling turpentine, called *caraña* and probably derived from the candlewood tree, was used by the Indians in embalming (a skill well-developed between here and Colombia); it was one of the more valuable intertribal trade items, a calabashful being "worth the same as a tapir."

Presumably the reference here is to Baird's tapir. The thorough taming of the animal described in this passage, and its implied abundance, are of special interest considering the fact that the tapir is now so very shy, and listed as being in danger of extinction. Some twenty years ago, I was served tapir meat in a Térraba household. Although I have met nobody who claimed to have killed one lately, on several recent occasions I have seen tapir hoofs in Guaymí houses where they are kept as trophies.

Peccaries have now been replaced by domesticated Old World pigs which are now feral in coastal parts of the forest near households; pigs also thrive on Escudo de Veraguas which now has no permanent human residents.

Throughout the 16th century (following Columbus's landing here) gold and slaves were the main interests of the Spanish in this area. Seeing many gold ornaments being worn by the natives, the Spanish assumed that there were rich mines in the vicinity and established several mining settlements. The results were disappointing: although the Indians did obtain small amounts of the gold by washing sands along local rivers, the larger quantity had been received in trade from northwestern Colombia. The Spaniards soon robbed the Indians of their gold and looted the richer Indian graves in the neighborhood. A partial depopu-

Collared peccary, Panama. (R. Buchsbaum)

Baird's tapir. Panama. (R. Buchsbaum)

lation of Veraguas by slavers followed. By the end of the century, Spanish interest in the area had waned. Nevertheless, in the 17th century, the area (even the islands in Almirante Bay which were easily approached by sea and frequently visited by the Spanish) was still well-settled by Indians. From the Río Tarire to Escudo de Veragua more than seventy leagues eastward, the country was described as pleasant, tranquil, and rich, not only in gold but in the products of agriculture. (The demographic changes described above and in the following paragraphs are based upon Léon Fernández 1881-1907, Vols. IV and V; for detail see Gordon, 1969).

Franciscan missionaries working around Almirante Bay collected considerable demographic information at the end of the 17th century. In these years they undertook a great program of transferring Indians from the western Bocas del Toro area to the Pacific slopes of Costa Rica and Panama, giving as their reasons the inter-tribal wars which kept the area in turmoil, and the raids of the Nicaraguan Miskito Indians—allies of the English. (The various Indian settlements of the Almirante Bay area have been mapped, using the detailed records of the Franciscans: Thiel, 1892).

Gold figure unearthed by a Guaymí in a garden in the Cricamola Valley. No evidence has yet been found that the early inhabitants of Bocas del Toro Province themselves had metallurgical skills. Most of the gold artifacts found here by the Spanish were in Indian graves and may have been traded in from the Pacific slope, especially from the area now known as Veraguas Province where exceptionally fine gold artifacts have been found at Coclé. But there too the evidence points to southern origins: "metal work [*in gold*] indicates that the Coclesanos were in touch with the Sinú tribe of Colombia whose products they *imported and copied*" (Lothrop, 1937, p. 70). Winged figures such as the one shown above are found along the Caribbean coast from Colombia to the Mayan area. They are said to be stylized eagles. Columbus carried on a brisk trade with the natives in such "eagles" and other gold ornaments, as he and his party passed along the south shores of Chiriquí Lagoon.

Historical Population Changes: Extinction of Tribes and Partial Abandonment of the Area

SIXTEENTH CENTURY documents refer to a settlement of Nahua-speaking Indians, known as the Sigua, in this area. Whether these "Aztecs" were here before the arrival of Europeans, or were brought from Mexico as mercenary warriors by the Spanish, has been a subject of debate (Lothrop, 1942). A slow incursion of northern peoples into the South American cultural realm appears to have been underway at the time of European discovery; the Sigua may have been an advance outpost of this invasion. Although Nahua-speakers survived here well into Colonial times, and some intermarried with the Térraba, there is no sign of them now except for a name: Térraba and Bribri, when speaking their own languages, call mestizos "Sigua."

The Changuinola River basin and the northern part of Almirante Bay, including Isla Colón (Toja), were the 16th century territory of the Térraba, then probably the most powerful group in the area. To the northwest of the Térraba lived the Talamancas and Cabégara; their neighbors on the southeast were the Changuena, living on the southern tributaries of the Changuinola River. One of these tributaries still appears on modern maps as the "Changuena." To the southeast of the Changuena, along the west side of Almirante Bay, were the Dorasque and to the south and east of the Dorasque, around Chiriquí Lagoon, were the Guaymí.

At the end of the 17th century, some of the Térraba were induced by Franciscan missionaries to cross to the Pacific slope of the sierra to the plains of Hato Viejo (today Buenos Aires in Costa Rica) to escape the depredations of their unconverted neighbors, the Changuena and the Talamancan Bribri. In 1705, a settlement of Térraba already existed on the Pacific slopes and there were plans to bring in 600 more of the tribe. The inhabitants of the Río Teribe Valley are probably descendants of Térraba who did not join the movement, or of some who later returned to their homeland.

By the end of the 17th century, the number of Térraba was much reduced. In 1697, the Franciscan missionaries counted 1,300 on the mainland and 800 on the island of Toja, 2,100 in all. Other accounts published in 1707 and 1709 give the total as 2,000.

Several modern Térraba folk tales refer to times when the Talamanca, Miskito and Changuena were all warring against them. They are now on good terms with the Bribri: a few influential Indians upriver are Bribri, married to Térraba women, including their *sukia,* that is their witch doctor or medicine man. (The word *sukia,* commonly used among Indians and non-Indians throughout this area, is probably of Miskito origin, established during the period of Miskito incursions southward along this coast.) Such circumstances bear out Gabb's statement that the Bribri were victors in wars at the beginning of the 19th century, and that the Térraba have since been treated by the Bribri as a subject people (Gabb, 1875, p. 448). True, the two languages are related and the two are otherwise culturally similar, but it is probable that they have become even more alike recently as a result of Bribri dominance.

The Changuena, who have only recently become extinct, were for a time the next most numerous of the tribes living near the embayment, the number being given as at least 3,650 in 1706. An account written in 1703 places their number at 11,000, though the writer may have exaggerated: he was asking for military assistance to be used against them. There were said to be 5,000 in 1707 and 1709. A few Changuena survived as late as 1875 (Gabb, 1975, p. 487).

The Guaymí, farther from the missions on Almirante Bay, were less carefully counted than were the other tribes and little historical information about them is available. At the beginning of the 18th century, their number was estimated at close to 8,000. at 1700 AD

Reference is made in these same times to the Dorasque Indians, but no estimate of their numbers appears; presumably they were not numerous then, and have long since become extinct. In short, the total Indian population living around Almirante Bay and its islands was some 7,000, not counting the Dorasque, a few Siguas on the lower Changuinola, and the Guaymí, who were actually mostly around the Lagoon and eastward. An Indian rebellion brought most of the Franciscan missionary activity to a halt around 1709.

Thus by the early 18th century there had been a marked reduction in tribal diversity, and with partial abandonment of the Province, the considerable area of Indian gardens and regrowth was reclaimed by heavy forest. Nevertheless, as evidence of how productive the aboriginal economy had been, some 250 years later, in 1960, the population of even the most densely settled part of the Province (that is the western part, including Bocas del Toro and the Company towns of Almirante, Changuinola, etc.) was but slightly greater than in the earlier century.

4

GUAYMI FOREST USE

Early Settlement of Western Caribbean Forests

THE TROPICAL rainforest excels in the production of organic material. With a year-long growing season, abundant water, and photosynthesis at a maximum, one may expect a thriving agriculture. The production of vegetable material, as measured by the annual yield in dry weight of organic matter or calories per hectare, is not surpassed by other land areas. Nevertheless, a large part of this country is quite unproductive of organic materials suitable for human use, an old and well-known paradox. From the standpoint of human settlement and land use, a basic problem is to direct this growth potential to the production of useful calories without destroying the rainforest as a functioning ecosystem.

True, soils derived from recently deposited alluvium and volcanic ash in the area are now generally productive, and commercial agriculture is practiced very successfully upon them, though with no regard for the conservation of existing ecological conditions. However, on the zonal soils of the much larger interfluve areas, the results of agriculture have been disappointing. Because of its generally degrading effects on the physical environment, it is unlikely that cattle raising will prove to be a successful form of land use in the long run, even in strictly economic terms. On the other hand, dense populations have developed in the past in rainforest areas where soils are neither volcanic nor alluvial. Some of these were the Zenú in lowland northwestern Colombia; the Coiba-Cueva peoples in eastern Panama, whose soils were derived from deeply weathered sedimentary and igneous rocks; the Indians of Bocas del Toro Province; and the Mayans on the limestone soils of Yucatán. Archaeological studies suggest densities of well over one hundred persons per km^2 in parts of the Mayan area, but without great urban concentrations. Indeed, relatively high densities may be needed for effective control and use of the vegetation while practicing their methods of tropical arboriculture as described below.

Archaeological and historical evidence indicate that a large part of the rainforests of Meso-America was once inhabited, some of it for centuries, and by dense populations. Discussing the early colonization of western Caribbean forests Spinden (1928, pp. 650-1) refers to a lost art of settlement, as practiced by the Zenú in lowland northern Colombia and by the Quimbaya of the middle Cauca Valley, "Where the humid tropics were temporarily conquered after the manner of the Mayas." Speaking of the Mayan settlement of the rainforest of Yucatán, he writes:

> We know from their calendar that the Mayas were established in rainy regions as early as the seventh century before Christ. ... Then the adaptation to the forest zone in the Maya area took place, and the great economic success of this led to the conquest of forest areas elsewhere in Mexico and Central America, and the West Indies. ... From the archaeological evidence the first Empire appears to have been one of the most densely peopled parts of the world.

Spinden may be wrong as to the source and direction of such "conquest" but the Maya and the Zenú did indeed use the forest-covered parts of their lands similarly. The art has not been lost; it survives in an impoverished form among Zenú descendants in Colombia and among the Maya themselves, and to a marked extent among the Panamanian tribes described here. Present Guaymí use of forest lands—and in lesser detail Térraba and Bókata use—are discussed on the following pages.

Cultural Differences and the Assessment of Forest Resources

OF THE THOUSANDS of species present in this rainforest only a small number enter into modern commerce, and that number (now almost exclusively lumber trees) is decreasing. Most species are too dispersed and inaccessible to be considered valuable. But recognition of potential products is a matter of cultural perspective, and Indian assessments of forest resources differ fundamentally from those made by visitors from the commercial world outside; the Guaymí's number of harvestable species is the larger by far.

Consider an example of resource assessment from a modern commercial standpoint, made characteristically in terms of exportable lumber trees: in virgin forest " ... there may be less than one harvestable individual of a particular species per hectare [2.47 acres] on an average, and the same hectare may contain up to 100 or more different species." (L.E. Eeckhout, 1953). That is, less than one out of a hundred tree species is useful.

But there is a more extreme case: while Indian land use developed with an emphasis upon multiplicity of products, modern agriculture has an opposite trend. Thus, from the viewpoint of the grazing industry this rainforest contains no significant resources whatever. It simply occupies space which can be put to profitable use with but a single product—cattle.

1. Useful Forest Plants

The following are a few of the forest plants used by the Guaymí. The plants are particularly important to families on new homesteads in the forest, but are also often used by Guaymí when they are travelling or hunting:

Bateo, Carapa sp. Lower Rîo San Pedro. The Guaymî make oil from the seed; and the fruit, which ripens in November-December, is eaten by the agouti and other wild animals. *Bateo,* is an important commercial lumber tree. The fruits pop, like those of the sandbox tree, when they open.

bateo *Carapa* sp.
An edible oil is extracted from the seeds. The tree's lumber is also valuable.

bejuco real ?
The thin stems of this liana are pliant, tough and durable. They are of great importance as a binding material in building houses.

candlewood tree *Trattinnickia aspera*
Latex has medicinal and other uses.

canjura *Gnetum leyboldii*
A liana; its large, pecan-like seeds have edible kernels.

chutra *Protium panamensis*
Useful latex.

conga palm *Oenocarpus panamanus*
Leaves used for house thatch.

dwarf palm *Chamaedorea* sp.
The inner parts of new shoots are edible.

forest cacao *Theobroma bernoulli*
Edible seeds.

forest plum *Maripa panamensis*
Tall shrub of forest and forest edges. The yellow plum-sized fruit contains an edible dark, sweet fluid around its seeds.

ground palm *Geonoma simplicifronds*
The leaves of this short palm are used in making temporary shelters.

granadilla *Passiflora vitifolia*
A liana with edible fruits. This passionflower, with large scarlet flowers, grows on sun bathed tree banks facing streams and pathways.

guamo del monte *Inga* sp.
A streamside tree; the sweet pulp around the seeds is eaten.

jirote palm *Socratea* ?
The split trunks are used for house floors.

macanguey palm *Attalea allennii*
The kernels of the prune-sized seeds are eaten raw.

manaca palm *Scheelea* sp.
The kernels of the egg-sized, coconut-like seeds are eaten raw.

mayo ?
A tree with yellow cherry-size edible fruit.

milk tree *Conma macrocarpa*
Tree with edible fruit.

monkey pot *Couratari panamensis*
The fruit capsule is hollow and tubular; it is used as a container; for instance as a salt cellar it is kept in the ashes at the edge of hearths.

negrito *Ecclinusa guianensis*
A tree whose latex is useful for glue.

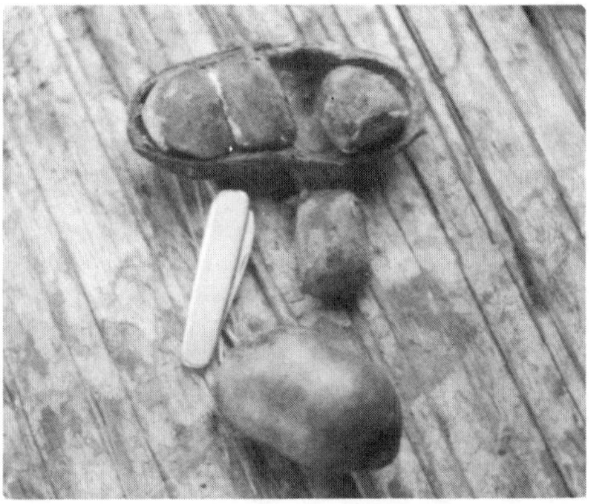

Ubere, a liana, *Dioclea* sp. The soft, heavy rhomboidal fruit pods and their large seeds are roasted and eaten. Lower stems of the lianas may be 7 to 10 cm. in diameter; several Guaymí join hands to hawl them down from the tree branches. In terms of yield, this is one of the most important forest food plants; each liana bears dozens of fruit pods.

nuomá ?
Tree with edible, orange-colored, rough-skinned fruit about the size of a litchi.

palmito *Welfia georgii*
The center of the crown is sweet and edible.

pigeon plum *Hirtella latifolia*
Tree, with small yellow edible fruit.

rancho palm *Synechanthus warscewiczianus*
The leaves of this waist-high palm are used in making roofs of temporary shelters, i.e. "ranchos."

red fungus ?
This frilled red fungus which grows on fallen tree trunks is dried and eaten.

sándi *Pseudolmedia spuria*
The tree's bark is used for barkcloth.

sapodilly *Manilkara bidentata*
Tree, bears sweet, edible fruit. The latex is made into rubber.

tapir palm *Geonoma* sp.
A waist-high palm; its whitish, fist-sized fruit, cooked, is important in times of food scarcity.

ubere *Dioclea pulchra* ?
A liana with a heavy rectangular pod containing large edible seeds.

Fruit and leaves of the *negrito, Ecclinusa guianensis,* a smooth-barked tree of the sapodilly family. The tree ripens fruit in both January and July, attracting many game animals. The latex, yellow and sticky, is used as glue.

water vine *Doliocarpus major*
A large liana, the stem of which grows several inches thick; a segment cut and upended yields a potable fluid which tastes like fresh water.

wild arrowroot ?
An apparently undescribed species in the Marantaceae, growing on shaded inland streambanks. Its root is edible.

wild banana *Heliconia latispatha*
Used for wrapping birds, frogs, lizards, etc. before roasting them over coals. One of the few *bihaos* which tolerates deep shade.

wild tama-tama *Inga goldmanii*
Medium-sized tree; the sweet pulp around its seeds is eaten.

yellow mombin *Spondias mombin*
Tree bearing tart yellow fruit.

zobágria *Maripa panamensis*
This forest liana is sometimes found draped over small trees at the edge of the forest and along paths, where its fruit can be easily reached. The yellow, plum-sized fruit contains an edible sweet dark syrup.

Among the more important useful plants in the forest are those used for fish poisoning and canoe making.

Fish poisoning shrubs and vines:

Amphidaysa sp. Rubiaceae
(Apparently a new species: Dr. John D. Dwyer, personal communication)

Paullinia fasciculata ? Sapindaceae
(Or possibly a new species: Dr. Thomas B. Croat, personal communication)

Piper darienense Piperaceae

Serjania pluvialiflorens Sapindaceae

Serjania sp. Sapindaceae
(A new species, or at least "apparently new to Panama": Ronald Liesner, personal communication.)

The leaves, bark and roots of fish-poisoning plants are chopped up and strewn in slow-moving water.

The bark of at least one tall forest tree is also used as fish poison. In Guaymí the tree is called **kévegua-guada.** The bark is chopped and ground on a stone mortar. It is one of the most potent poisons used, and is said to kill even shrimp.

In addition to the fish-poisoning plants listed above, at least one other species of *Serjania,* two other species of *Piper,* and another species of *Paullinia* are also used by the Guaymí. (The genus *Paullinia* is widely known for its fish-poisoning qualities.)

Trees for making dugout canoes include: johncrow wood, *kurutú, laurél,* sandbox, *santa maria,* and tropical cedar.

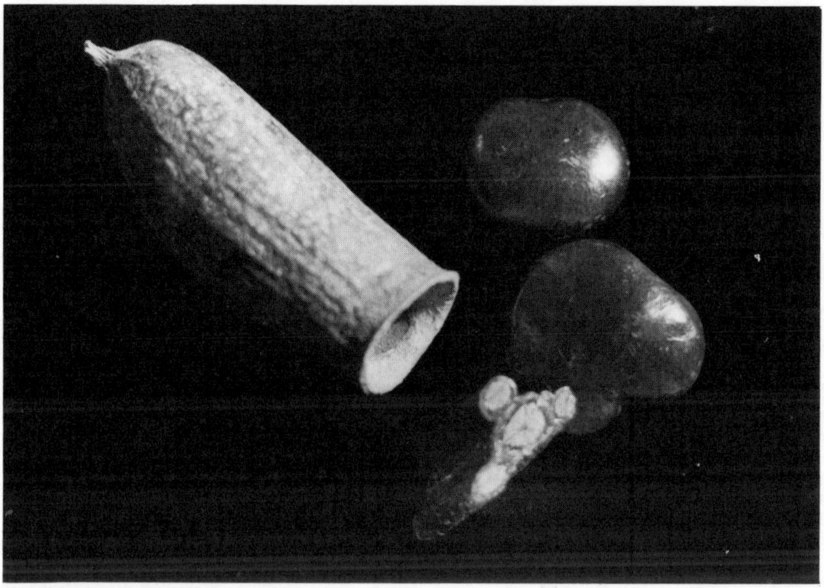

Fruit of the monkey pot tree, *Couratari panamensis* (left); Sea Beans, *Entada monostachya* (upper tight); segment of the typically multi-ply stem of **nióngra** Pallinia sp., a liana used as a fish poison (bottom).

The number of fish-poisoning plants and canoe-making trees identified by the Guaymí (and the lists are only partial) suggests the importance of streams as a source of food. In the settlement of uninhabited forest, use of these plants gives quick access to aquatic resources; in earlier times they were likely of even greater importance.

The lists do not include the numerous plants with medicinal uses.

Some of the trees listed above are also important as "hunting trees": Since trees of each species tend to grow scattered through the forest, when they bear fruit they often become well-separated congregation centers for feeding animals. For instance, peccaries, pacas and agoutis gather to eat the fruit of such trees as the *almendro, negrito, bateo, membrillo silvestre* and *membrillo del monte,*—or of lianas which various trees support, such as *canjura.* Birds collect in fruiting *pera* trees, etc. Hunters seek out such trees and wait for the animals, mornings and evenings.

2. Forest Animals Eaten by the Guaymí

The white-lipped peccary, brocket deer, tapir, and howler monkey are well-known Indian game animals elsewhere in tropical American forests. And these are hunted by the Guaymí too, along with less generally eaten large mammals such as the giant anteater and the sloth. Such large game may have been a more important source of food formerly than now—since in recent times some of these animals have become harder to find. But it is the smaller animal life of the forest that now provides food on a day-by-day basis; and this was probably true in the past as well. The following are among the more commonly eaten small animals:

Crested guans, Térraba pets *(above)*. The great curassow *(below)*. Species of the family Cracidae (curassows, guans, and chachalacas) are among the most hunted large game birds in Panama. They are often kept as pets by the Guaymí and Térraba, and flock together with the family chickens when called at feeding time.

Forest lizard, *Corytophanes cristatus.* (R. Buchsbaum)

Land crab. (R. Buchsbaum)

At least two species of forest lizard are eaten: the **u-grra** (*Corytophanes cristatus*), with fin-like structures on its head, and the **jilida** (*Anolis* sp.), a smaller lizard which puffs its throat out threateningly when alarmed.

Edible forest frogs include the following: the **ogungó** (*Eleutherodactylus gollmeri*), a medium-sized frog, its body being between four and five cm in length. Resting on the forest floor, it is easily mistaken for a dry leaf. The **nu-lu** (*Eleutherodactylus crassidigitus*) is also collected though it is so small—its body being only about two cm long—that it seems hardly worth bothering with. Like the lizards , these frogs are wrapped in green leaves and roasted.

The white land crab, considerably lighter in color than other land crabs, makes its burrows in moist soils under various types of plant cover—both forest and regrowth. Although especially common in lowlands, it is also found in hill country miles from shoreline. But wherever it burrows, the crab must return to the sea, annually, to spawn. And because of its great seaward migrations the crab is well-known, to Indians and other inhabitants, as well. Migration takes place in April and May, and during this time crabs are sometimes so numerous that the forest positively rustles with their movements. As they march through Indian clearings (the bellies of the females covered with yellow eggs), they are collected by the bagful. On occasion the crabs have been shipped to Colón for sale.

Of greater importance in remote inland forests are various of the river crab family (Pseudothelphusidae) which do not need to return to saltwater to spawn. One such crab, the **bu-lo** (unidentified), is much sought by the Guaymí for food; it is larger than the white land crab, with a dark brown carapace some five or six inches in length. Found in mountainous country it makes its burrows in undisturbed forest; and not necessarily in the immediate vicinity of running water. Not only does this crab not need to return periodically to the sea; it actually becomes more abundant the farther one goes from shoreline, being found high on the slopes of the Serrania de Tabasará. The Guaymí in remote forests also eat several much smaller crabs of the same family; (one specimen was identified as follows: "close to but not identical with *Ptychophallus tumimanus* ... may represent an undescribed species." (Dr. Austin B. Williams, Systematics Laboratory, National Museum of Natural History, Washington, D.C., personal communication).

In inland waters the following are the principal Indian food fishes: The most commonly caught, because it is present year around in all small tributaries throughout the forest, is a livebearer called **bidigá** (*Rivulus* sp.); this is probably the most important single food fish for inland Guaymí and Bókata. Another fish found far upstream as well as along the coast is the goby known as *tití* (*Sycidium* sp.). Fish poison is used to take such small fish in the streams. Larger fish are sometimes caught in wicker traps.

The largest of the upriver fish is the *bocachica* which may weigh several pounds. But it is hard to catch with traps because it usually stays in rapids and fast-flowing water. Fish poison cannot be used there and, since the *bocachica* rarely takes a baited hook, it is either speared or—more commonly—shot with bow and arrow.

All species of shrimp are eaten. One of the more common is the **nablá** (*Macrobrachium crenulatum*), caught by hand amongst the rocks in shallow water. Guaymí youngsters take up stones and pound larger rocks beneath which the shrimp have found cover. When the rocks are overturned, the stunned shrimp are easily caught.

One of the more important Indian aquatic food animals is a small, brown, water snail, called *chilile* in Spanish, which grows on rocks in shallow, running water. It ranges to the headwaters of the streams. Whole families of Guaymí can sometimes be seen harvesting the mollusk, filling small net carrying bags. The *chilile* is a major and persistent supply of protein since it can be collected at all seasons. To survive such heavy harvest pressure, the species must reproduce prodigiously.

Iguanas are killed along the lower banks of the rivers. A more important food lizard, because it is more common, is the well-known "Jesus-lizard", so called because it scampers over the surface of the water. Like the iguana, it lives on river banks. Next to the iguana, it is the largest local lizard and after the iguana, the Guaymí favorite. Also caught for food in the rivers are at least two freshwater turtle species.

Newly-gathered *chilile, Neritina clenchi.*This fresh water mollusk is a food of major importance to Guaymí and Bókata Indians. Discarded shells below.

Indian Silviculture and Arboriculture

A COMPLETE LIST of forest plants eaten by the Guaymí would be lengthy indeed. But inspection of the short list above shows that few are heavy producers of food calories; for example, good starch producers are scarce. Because they are widely scattered the listed plants can provide only a supplementary food supply for a dense human population. Even as seen by a knowledgeable Guaymí, useful materials are too dispersed in undisturbed forest to support a functioning human community. Change is necessary. Under Guaymí custom the needed change is an areal concentration of useful species within the forest, effected through various arboricultural and agricultural practices not sharply separable from each other.

Within the forest the peculiar distributions of some tree species suggest that they were not naturally disseminated; for example, those which appear in isolated groves at abandoned habitation sites—forming there what ecologists sometimes call "archaeological disclimaxes." Except under localized edaphic circumstances, such obvious close spacing is not common where there has been no human occupancy.

The extent of past human penetration and use of tropical forests is often underestimated; archaeological sites and scattered artifacts are common in areas which are now unsettled. Furthermore, along old Indian trails (myriads of which—used or abandoned—crisscross even remote parts of the forest) trees of certain species grow with unusual frequency. When catalogued, such effects turn out to be widespread. Indeed, one knowledgeable writer concluded that "there are no undisturbed forests in Central America" (Cook, 1909).

The following notes on plant distribution and Indian silviculture show that from Guatemala southward across the Isthmus, species composition of the rainforest was locally changed as a result of the subsistence activities of prehistoric human inhabitants. In Bocas del Toro Province tree distribution has been considerably altered well beyond the present sites of Indian agriculture.

1. Anomalous Tree Distributions in Unsettled Forest

About a mile up the Río San Pedro, an old Indian trail runs eastward to the coast at the head of Caño Blanco. The trail runs part of this distance through regrowth vegetation, but for a little over a kilometer it goes over heavily forested hills. This forest is relatively undisturbed: slopes are steep, and local Guaymí cannot remember a time when any of it was cleared for agriculture.

Accompanied by a Bocatoreño and a Guaymí to provide native tree names and, where possible, to help in collecting materials for further identification, I made a count of certain kinds of trees growing along this stretch. My companions named the trees by inspecting leaves, seeds, or flowers on the ground beneath, or by observing the texture of the bark and chopping into its flesh to note color and odor. Trees on either side of the trail—none more than fifteen meters from the trail itself—were named and counted. Following is a list of trees of whose identity my companions seemed certain, all of which yield products useful to the Guaymí:

Trees	**Number of Individuals**
milk tree (*pera*)	15
sapodilly (*nispero*)	7
sándí	5
bateo	3
chutra	2
santa Maria	2
kurutú	2
cascarillo	1
tawega	1
conga palm	1
macangue palm	1
jirote palm	1
mayo	1

The trunks of the trees counted ranged in diameter from about 15 cm to 1.5 m at shoulder height. Since small saplings were not counted and some trees were undoubtedly overlooked, the counts represent minimal values. The trunks of the 42 trees counted are in a strip about 30 m wide and a kilometer long; that is in an area of about three hectares.

In the lumberman's estimate quoted earlier, the total forest resource (i.e., lumbertrees) may be "less than one harvestable individual per hectare." Granted, the lumberman is looking at large and well-preserved trees only, but nevertheless the list shows how different is the Guaymí view of tree resources. In the Guaymí count tabulated above the number of useful trees averages over 14 per hectare. And, of course, the count disregards the many other useful plants (shrubs, lianas, etc.) within the surveyed area.

Of special interest here is the uncommonly high population densities of three trees, the milk tree, the sapodilly and the *sándi.* When first taking to the trail we left a cluster of Indian houses near the river: Four milk trees were counted almost immediately upon entering the forest, whereas few were counted toward the opposite end of the trail—that is in the part of the forest farthest from human settlement. In an attempt to establish a control, we tried a count away from the trail near its midpoint, in opposite directions. (Because of rough terrain it was not possible to move in a straight line for a full kilometer): Only one *sándi* was found, and no sapodilly; thus, the distribution of these two plants appears to be related to the trail. On the other hand, five milk trees were counted—leaving the latter tree's association with the trail less certain.

The milk tree is a tall, thick-trunked forest tree. The outer bark is only slightly rough, and unfurrowed. When this outer bark is cut away, a pink or salmon-colored underbark is exposed and a milky, slightly sweet latex begins to flow. The milk tree is said to be completely deciduous in May when it flowers. The flowers are red and tubular. The fruiting season is around October, at which time the bright green fruits litter the ground. The fruit, which contains black, bean-sized seeds buried in a white flesh, is prized by the Guaymí; animals also consume large quantities. The wood is very smooth and hard, and does not split easily. Wooden mortars are often made from it, e.g., those used for de-husking rice. The Guaymí occasionally plant the seeds in their gardens, but the seedlings will only grow in deep shade. Although the tree is more concentrated in some parts of the forest than in others, it rarely appears in regrowth—evidence that its concentration, if actually a result of Indian activities, took place solely within a forest environment. The dense populations of milk tree in Guaymí forests (in place more than 6 per hectare) are particularly interesting in view of the fact that the tree is scarcely known elsewhere in Panama (Ronald Liesner, Missouri Botanical Garden, personal communication).

The *sándi* is one of the largest forest trees, even larger than the milk tree. It bears a small, russet-colored fruit which is edible, but less tasty than that of the milk tree. Both trees have a smooth outer bark but the fleshy underbark of the *sándi* is yellowish rather than pink. Some say that the milky latex can be drunk in coffee but I have seen no such use of it; it is not sweet like that of the milk tree. The *sándi* is of major importance to the Guaymí and Bókata. Barkcloth, used for garments and sleeping pads, is made from the bark of young trees collected in the forest; such cloth was of vastly greater importance before store-bought clothing became available. Segments of the trunks or branches are beaten, for instance, with the back of a machete, with diagonal blows. The sticks are then upended and beaten again until the bark can be slipped off like a sleeve. Conservative Guaymí women still prefer bark cloth to cotton for some purposes. Some say the bark cloth is warmer than cotton and that it stretches more readily to fit the contours of the body. It is also preferred for pack straps. Piles of barkcloth are made in the upper San Pedro Valley, then carried in packs over the Tabasará Mountains to the Chiriquí slopes for sale to the savanna Guaymí. A similar barkcloth is made by the Chocó Indians at the eastern end of the Isthmus and in various other parts of tropical America. The "paper" used for Mayan writing was made from fig-family trees, as was the tapa of the Pacific Islanders. Wild pineapple often grows with *sándi* around archaeological sites, e.g., on shell mounds near Chiriquí Lagoon.

Sapodilly, or *nispero,* is one of the more generally useful of Guaymí trees. It has a very rough bark, which on older trees is divided into platelets about an inch thick. Although the platelets are lacking on young trees, their bark is rough, too, with longitudinal grooves. Both the fleshy part of the bark and the wood itself are quite red. When the bark is cut, the tree produces a milky latex which is now the major source of rubber coming out of this forest; the rubber is a balata, a non-elastic rubber with various industrial uses. The latex is coagulated and put on a board in the sun to dry. Blocks of sapodilly rubber are picked up by coastal boats and carried to markets in Colón. The trunks of most large trees growing near the coast are marked with diagonal machete scars, often well above the ground because collectors nowadays use irons to climb the trees. (Sapodilly latex is sometimes adulterated here with the abundant latex of the milk tree; the mixture can be detected, because it burns poorly with a very smoky flame). The sweet, gummy fruit is a favorite among Indians and Bocatoreños alike, and the Guaymí make it into a fermented drink. The fruit also attracts many forest animals. The wood will burn when freshly cut. The tree gives Sapodilly Point its name.

Even denser concentrations of useful tree species than those along the trail to Río Caño can be found in unsettled forests elsewhere, for example on Sándi Hill near Palo Blanco. The hill is almost completely covered with tall forest, through which several trails extend connecting Guaymí households in the surrounding area. Near the hill's flat crest there is a great concentration of *sándi.* For example, on one slope some 26 *sándi* trees, young and old, are crowded together in an area no more than 60 yards long and 40 yards wide, intermixed with only a few other tree species—including several large milk trees. In the immediately surrounding forest the fruit of *membrillo del monte,* a species of *Inga* falls in such quantities that it almost covers parts of the trail. *Mayo* trees are also especially numerous; in July the ground beneath them is littered with their edible fruits, usually much trampled by peccaries.

In the regrowth forest found on sites which are still easily recognizable as having been used for agriculture populations of useful trees are yet more concentrated, as described below.

2. Pre-historic Tribal Exchange of Plants

The large number of trees and shrubs disseminated across the Isthmus of Panama in pre-Columbian times indicates the role of pre-historic man in extending ranges and in modifying the character of species. Such plants are evidence, too, of an extensive aboriginal cultural exchange between the Americas, both in themselves and through cultural traits associated with their use. Probably most have their origins in tropical forests, though in many cases their wild progenitors are uncertain. Several, widely cultivated in prehistoric America, have become important economic plants: cacao and manioc are examples. Others transported across or onto the Isthmus, and still cultivated by present-day Panamanian Indians, include: the tree calabash, the peach palm, and the avocado; less generally known are *membrillo,* patashte, and monkey's head. That this part of Panama is not within the natural range of these plants is indicated by the fact that they occur here only under cultivation or in association with old Indian habitation sites.

The identical use made of some wild species from tribe to tribe also suggests exchange of knowledge even though the plants themselves, being native throughout much of the area, may not have been traded or transported over long distances: The *ceiba* tree, for instance, was planted in groves by both the Maya and the Zenú, and was sacred to both. But of more significance here is the peculiar distribution of certain food-producing trees which grow untended within Central American forests.

Two especially important trees of the Mayan area were the chicle, or *zapote chico* (*Manilkara sapota,* formerly known as *Achras sapota*) and the breadnut, or *ramón* (*Brosimum alicastrum*). The "chicle and breadnut trees are found in special abundance among the ruins of the Maya cities and are largely responsible for the archaeological discoveries of the last half-century." (Cook, 1935, p. 615).

In one forest association of the Mayan area in Peten, chicle is described as the dominant tree (Bartlett, 1936, p. 15):

> The general prevalence of *zapote chico* (*Achras sapota*) throughout so great an area, and the apparent fact that the vast majority of the trees seem to belong to a very old age class suggest that the factor of human occupation of the land was all-important in determining this major plant association. It is probable that the usefulness of the very sweet fruit as a food in a sugarless diet may have led the Maya to spare the *zapote* when other trees were destroyed in the clearing of land for planting annual crops.

Not only is the tree the source of chicle, but beams made of its fine, durable wood were much used in Mayan architecture. Discussing the occurrence of this same tree in Costa Rica, Standley (1937, p. 905) remarks: "Although the trees are often found in apparently primeval forest in southern Central America, there is some doubt as to whether they are truly native here, or rather relics of ancient cultivation." The similar concentrations of the closely related sapodilly tree, or *nispero,* in Guaymí forests has been noted above.

Of the occurrence of the breadnut, or *ramón,* in the Mayan area (Lundell 1933, p. 72) writes:

> I have found groves of the *ramón* tree (*Brosimum alicastrum*) covering every Southern culture ruin which I have visited, and it is no mere coincidence that this species is so abundant there. Of the other trees, cacao and *mamey* were doubtless of the greatest importance as additional tree crops, for they also bear fruit in the dry season. It is probable that these trees and many others which are now found in the region also grew in some of the plazas and streets, providing both shade and food.

The seeds of the breadnut are still gathered by modern Mayas "for making their native bread when stocks of maize run low." (Cook, 1935, p. 615).

Similarly, the Térraba describe the breadnut as being among their oldest and most traditional foods. It is often grown near their houses; the young seedlings are easily identified, pulled up and transplanted. Since the breadnut is saved in forest clearing operations, it is very common around Térraba settlements. The dark colored fruits, which are somewhat larger than a coffeeberry, ripen in April and May. The wood burns green. (Some of the specimens which I collected appear to belong to a closely related species, *Brosimum terrabanum,* which also has been collected northward on Mayan sites. For instance, W.S. Schipp notes on a specimen preserved in the University of California Herbarium that he collected it on "Mayan mounds, Cockscomb Mts.; 500 ft., alt. 152 m, June 6, 1930.)

The mamey (*Mammea americana*) was probably also spread southward: speaking of the mamey in Costa Rican forests Standley (1937, p. 708) notes that it is " ... possibly native in some regions but more probably introduced." I have not seen it in the forests of Bocas del Toro Province.

After exhaustive study of forests and agriculture in tropical America, O.F. Cook (1935, p. 615) questioned that ancient Mayan civilization could have been "supported by a migratory 'milpa' agriculture like that of the present day, calling for a new forest clearing every year to grow the family maize crop." He suggested that the dense population may have been supported over centuries instead by "long-lived hardwood tree crops." (Cook, 1935, p. 616). The importance of the breadnut as a Mayan tree crop has been re-emphasized in more recent studies (e.g. Puleston, 1971, p. 330).

Such a system of forest modification and use may become more practicable as human population increases, because with many hands manual selection of the vegetation on a plant by plant basis can be intensified and elaborated. Maintenance of a productive forest probably demands a relatively dense population. In the Mayan area prehistoric population densities upward of 193 per km^2 have been estimated. As noted above, historical sources also describe denser forest populations in Bocas del Toro Province at Conquest time than at present.

3. Introduction of the Machete

The Mayan culture is sometimes described as being unique among high civilizations, thriving upon a shifting, milpa-type agriculture in a tropical forest environment. However, the term "shifting" clearly does not apply to terraced parts of the Mayan rainforest such as those in British Honduras. As Lundell (1933) points out:

> That a shifting type of agriculture, such as the milpa system, would be employed in a terraced area is unbelievable. The building of stone retaining walls and the filling-in with soil call for an investment in labor which would not be expanded for a form of agriculture where the land would be abandoned for eight to twelve years after one or two years. Terracing indicates continued occupation of land and at least a form of semi-permanent agriculture.

Another term which is sometimes used, "slash-and-burn agriculture" cannot appropriately be applied to pre-Columbian America; the Indians of Panama (like the Maya), having no metal tools, did no slashing. The whole tree-gardening complex discussed below is part of an older system which, though it includes a long-term fallow cycle, hardly fits the usual descriptions of shifting agriculture, much less slash-and-burn. The peach palm, for example, a major Guaymí crop, requires over six years to mature and may be continuously harvested for some seventy years. Other garden trees are similarly long-lived.

Clearing wet evergreen forest without metal cutting tools would clearly have been a slow and laborious process. Indian forest clearing was, and still is, relatively gradual, selective, and incomplete. Considering the cutting equipment (stone axes) which they possessed before arrival of the Europeans, it seems all but impossible that the Indians could have cleared, and kept clear, enough land for agriculture. One wonders how they even began such an operation—that is, how the earliest clearings were made and settlement begun. Several old Guaymí, asked how they would approach the problem of clearing a patch of forest without a machete, said they they would begin by seeking out and setting fire to those trees whose wood burns without being dried.

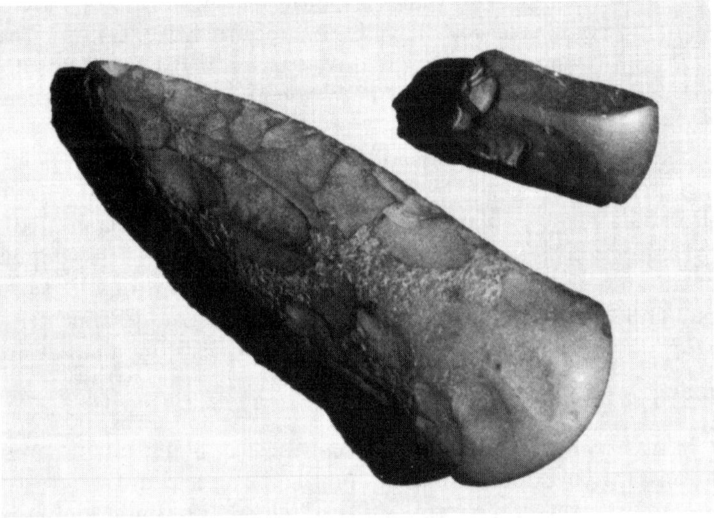

Ground-stone axes such as the larger one shown (about 25 cm in length) were probably used in forest clearing- for killing trees, by bruising the cambium bark-layer. The smaller, flat-based stone wedge may have been used in splitting logs.

Since, aside from such stone products as these, Guaymí lithic industry was poorly developed I have described their early economy as "biotechnic." This description still applies. (No metal artifacts are manufactured. Although metal implements, e.g. machetes, axes, and cooking ware are now widely used, they are imported.) Today lithic and ceramic artifacts have largely disappeared, modern craft products being almost entirely of animal and vegetable origin.

Guaymí fish poisons are made of pounded bark and leaves; it was perhaps during the period of earliest forest clearing, with its widespread bruising of tree and liana bark, that many such poisons were discovered.

Take the *almendro* for example: it is one of the taller forest trees, with a smooth, light-colored bark and a buttressed trunk. The wood is so hard that the tree cannot be felled using a machete; for that matter, it is very difficult to fell with an axe. On the other hand, one need only make a bruise in the bark along a buttress, lay burning coals against it and, given two rainless days, the tree will burn through and topple. Without rain, the fire will burn on, consuming even the branches of the fallen tree. In rainy weather a log will sometimes smolder for weeks.

Below is a list of the principal species which can thus be easily felled; young trees are additionally attractive because their branches can be torn off as a ready source of household fuel—a major consideration for survival in these humid forests:

Trees Whose Wood Burns When Freshly Cut

aceituño	?
alcareto	?
almendro	*Dipteryx panamensis*
bribri	*Inga punctata*
chutra	*Protium panamense*
cocoita	?
jabona	*Lacunaria panamensis*
kurutú	*Parkia sp.*
nispero	*Manilkara bidentata*
raska	*Licania hypoleuca*
santa maria	?

Of these trees the *kurutú* and *santa maría* are used for making dugout canoes. They were probably of special value here before metal cutting tools were available; fire could be used in hollowing out their logs—a procedure still practiced by the Guaymí in making wooden mortars for hulling rice.

The felling of but a few such giant trees would make small plots available for a house site and the beginnings of agriculture.

How could pre-Columbian Indians, using only fire and blunt stone axes, have significantly changed tree distribution within such humid and massive forests? Selection was probably done mainly at the seedling stage—the most efficient time, when cutting tools are least needed: The overall effort required to control the forest is least if applied at this time. It is easier to break off seedlings then to fell grown trees, and knee-high seedlings can be easily plucked from the loose mold. In the long run, selection at this stage makes for the greatest total yield of food and useful organic materials, since little solar energy—in short supply near the floor of the forest—is wasted upon unused growth.

The introduction of the machete by Europeans produced a major technological revolution and greatly changed the character of Indian forest use. Iron tools have now been in use here for several centuries; machetes and axes were already listed among the principal items traded to the Indians of Bocas del Toro in the late 17th century (Léon Fernández, 1881-1907, Vol. IV, p. 369). In a sense the Iron Age never came for the peoples native to the Americas: despite development of sophisticated metallurgical skills in some areas, no native tribes ever took to iron-making when that metal was made known to them; the Indians' complete dependence upon others for iron and associated trade items, from Conquest-time to the present, has been a significant factor in their acculturation.

In pre-machete times, plants had to be dealt with individually, felling a few trees at a time, destroying or transplanting seedlings, etc. After the arrival of the machete, old silvicultural practices were modified; larger and less well-sorted quantities of vegetation were dealt with. Nevertheless, even with his machete the Guaymí forest-farmer continues old selective habits; seldom without the tool as he travels, he lops off, almost unconsciously, unwelcome plants—a category which seldom includes useful species.

Using the machete, much more extensive clearings can be made with a reduced investment of labor. Larger amounts of slash are produced and burned, making it possible to kill most plant cover over sizeable tracts. Selective treatment is more difficult and although the Guaymí still preserve plants in the clearing process, survival of such plants is probably more a matter of chance now than formerly. The careful attention to individual plants and animals characteristic of the neolithic American agriculturist has diminished. It is because of the machete that Térraba (and to a lesser extent Guaymí), agriculture is coming to be similar to milpa, or shifting agriculture. And this is especially so where rice and other commercial crops are grown.

Térraba plantain and banana gardens in forest clearing along the Río Teribe. Large clearings such as this, sharp-edged with high forest walls and few trees left standing, probably were not a feature of the aboriginal landscape before introduction of the machete.

Morley (1947, p. 148) believes that the machete was not in fact beneficial to Mayan agriculture:

> A second-year *milpa* has far more weeds and vines in it than the high bush [a local name for forest cover]. This is due principally to the modern method of weeding with a machete. In ancient times, seeds were pulled out by the roots and the consequent scattering of seeds was held to a minimum; today however, weeds are cut with a sweep of the machete and the seeds scattered in every direction.

Old fields will, of course, have more low growth and weeds than the forest, not simply because of use of the machete; it is because most weedy vegetation is strongly heliophile that the ground surface in evergreen forest is almost without such undergrowth. This point aside, it is claimed that continuously cultivated milpas sustain yields about four times as long when the weeding is done by hand as when done with the machete (Morley, 1947, p. 153). I think that among ancient forest farmers the role of controlled shade in suppressing these weeds was considerable and that an overstorey of trees was arranged accordingly.

4. Trees Left Standing in Clearing the Forest

Even in these days of larger-scale felling using machetes and axes, and by burning (where saving individual trees is often inconvenient) the Guaymí, following old silvicultural practices, systematically spare various useful species—among them the following:

bateo	*Carapa* sp.
candlewood tree	*Trattinnickia aspera*
chutra	*Protium panamense*
conga palm	*Welfia georgii*
jira palm	*Socratea durissima*
jirote palm	*Socratea* ?
johncrow wood	*Vochysia ferruginea*
kurutú	*Parkia* sp.
laurél	*Cordia alliodora*
sándi	*Pseudolmedia spuria*
sapodilly	*Manilkara bidentata*
santa maría	?
tropical cedar	*Cedrela* sp.
wild tama-tama	*Inga goldmanii*
yellow mombin	*Spondias mombin*

Typically in a new clearing in the Río San Pedro Valley, there are scattered huge sapodilly and yellow mombin trees, a few *sándi*, numerous tall, spindly *jirote* and a smaller number of *conga* palms. The *sándi* is less frequently saved now than formerly because barkcloth is losing its importance. The saving of other trees (for example, trees for canoe-making) varies from place to place depending upon need. Strangler figs flourish on isolated trees, e.g. on the yellow mombin. Several of these large trees live on through several garden-fallow cycles; hence in places sapodilly populations are much concentrated. For example, along the coastal trail between the mouths of the Río Chiriquí and Río San Pedro sapodilly is actually the most common forest tree: that area has been so long and intentionally used that, as a Toreño resident put it, forest there is "not just second growth, but twenty-second growth."

Four species of palm play an important part in Guaymí arboriculture and tree gardening: the *guagara, jirota, jira,* and *conga* palms. All are both planted by the Guaymí and saved in their forest clearing operations.

The *guagara* grows mainly on moist lowland, though not actually in wet swamps like the raphia palm. In its first years, the palm appears to be stemless, but eventually it rises and develops a single trunk. In January, the fruit matures in large clusters. At the same time newly-forming fruit is present in sheaths on the tree. In July, mature fruit is also present. Thus, there are at least two fruiting seasons. In fact all four of these palms (*guagara, jirote, jira,* and *conga*) appear to bear fruit over much of the year; I also found mature fruit on the *jirote, jira,* and *conga* in both January and July. Since all of these palms bear heavily, especially the *guagara,* their fruits are important animal food. *Guagara* seeds are enclosed in a horny cover; they are about the size of a horse chestnut and a favorite food of both white-lipped and collared peccaries, and of squirrels. The sheath, which covers the large clusters of young fruit, is another useful item. It is cone-shaped and made up of meshed fibers. Carefully stretched, the sheaths are very expandable. The Guaymí stretch them and make dip nets in only a few minutes, fastening the open end of the cone to a frame made simply by bending a withe into a circle. If a sheath tears, it can be easily mended with thread. The Guaymí also wear the sheaths in what looks like a "stocking cap" at stick games. The *guagara* is the most important thatch-palm in low country.

The *jirote* is a stilt palm. The stilts are close together and rise somewhat higher than a man's head. Unlike the *jira* palm, it has either no prickles on its stilts, or but a few scattered, blunt ones. The *jirote* is found in old forest, sometimes along with the lower-growing *conga* palm; both are conscientiously protected during forest clearing. In places the *jirote* rises nearly to the upper forest canopy since spindly specimens, which are some 60 to 80 feet tall, are typically scattered around in newly-formed clearings.

Somewhat shorter than the *jirote,* the *jira* palm also has a smooth trunk rising above stilts about as tall as a man. But the stilts are more widely spread than are those of the *jirote* (which palm it much resembles), and covered with short, conical, woody prickles; in fact, pieces of the stilts are sometimes used for ready-made coconut graters.

Next to the peach palm, the *jira* is the most common palm in low-country Guaymí gardens. In undisturbed, or but-slightly disturbed, forest the *jira* is rather widely scattered. Forests in which it does grow plentifully are usually advanced secondary growth. (The other three palms are commonly seen in mature forest). In the Río San Pedro-San Pedrito area, the *jira* is especially a

Guaymí garden and regrowth tract in the San Pedro Valley. The taller trees, mainly *jirote*-palm and *nispero,* left standing when the clearing was made, show the height of the lower canopy in the original forest.

palm of Guaymí gardens and *rastrojo.* Its seedlings are often planted and the trees survive for a long time in the regrowth when gardens are abandoned. The trees are always left standing when the *rastrojo* is again cleared for planting. Thus, human planting and selective clearing are a major factor in explaining its distribution. On the other hand, the palm is probably also spread by birds. Although the seeds are very hard, with only a thin fleshy covering, they are eaten by both the keel-billed toucan and the collared aricari (both of which are, significantly, themselves birds of regrowth, tree garden, and forest edge; that is to say, the distribution of both the birds and the palm are associated with clearing activities). As the seeds of the *jira* are said to pass through the alimentary tracts of these large birds (perhaps they are regurgitated instead?), the palm is likely partly disseminated, in this way.

The *jira* is the choice palm for making Guaymí, Bókata, and Térraba house floors and this is its principal use. The trunks are split and "unrolled" to make a slat flooring. Though the slats, separated by cracks, usually remain attached to each other by splinters, the rounded outer surfaces of the slats, placed uppermost, are smooth, pliant, and comfortable for bare feet. The impermeable leaf sheaths, folded up something like a cardboard box, are among the most common containers for carrying water.

The *jira* is most abundant in the coastal hills; but its seeds are also carried well inland to higher country where good floor-making palms are scarce, and planted there in Guaymí tree gardens.

The *conga* palm grows to some 25 or 30 feet in height. It has no stilts and the trunk is belted with circular depressions, actually old leaf scars. The leaf scapes are much longer than are those of the *jira* or *jirote. Conga* is common in old forest, where it rises to about one-half the height of the upper canopy. Growing naturally, it is more of an inland palm than the *guagara,* but it is also planted for use as thatch in hills and along the coast where the *guagara* is absent. For example, in a single Guaymí tree garden on low hills near the mouth of Río San Pedrito I counted a dozen *conga* palms. The *conga* grows best if planted in the partial shade of other trees. As with the *jira,* its seeds are carried into the mountains to be planted in Guaymí gardens there.

Jira-palms, *Socratia durissima,* in Guaymí garden, Río San Pedro. The fruit ripens at least twice during the year. (Note that the fruiting clusters are at different stages of development.)

Genipap, *Genipa americana,* a small tree. Its sap was used extensively in aboriginal American tropics as a dark blue body paint; it is used by the Guaymí for dyeing carrying bags. Formerly it was left standing in the clearing of forests, but is now usually felled.

In July and August, lavender spots produced by flowering *almendro* trees can be seen throughout the forested hills of Térraba country. Since the Térraba protect this legume when clearing forest (as noted above it is extremely flammable) the trees rise in concentrated populations above regrowth and gardens, serving as shade trees for cacao and other plants. As its Spanish name suggests, the fruit somewhat resembles a large almond; and like the almond, it has a husk that splits and breaks off. The fruit is produced in large quantities and attracts peccaries, agoutis, etc. when it falls. The hard seeds are broken on stones and the kernels roasted and eaten or used in making oil. As commercial foods become available to the Térraba *almendro* fruit is less used, but in remote Indian households the kernels, ground and made into a chocolate-like drink, are still common fare. The *almendro,* like the breadnut, is one of the more important trees in Térraba arboriculture; its seedlings, easily recognized with the large, distinctive seeds still clinging to them, are often transplanted.

The *almendro* is also occasionally seen (and planted) in Guaymí country but in no such concentrations as those found in the Térraba area; nor was I able to find breadnut growing in the Guaymí area.

Among the Guaymí a favorite tree for making dugout canoes is the johncrow wood. The boat is one of the few native artifacts whose importance has definitely not decreased of late: throughout most of the province dugouts are the only transport vehicle; among Bocatoreños the canoes are usually fitted with outboard motors. Very large dugouts are much in demand for hauling produce along the coast, and there is a constant search for suitable canoe trees. Deep in the forest one occasionally comes on a trunk of a felled tree, rough-hewn to canoe shape; such canoe-logs are later dragged to the nearest water and floated downstream for finishing. Where other canoe trees are scarce, the Guaymí spare the johncrow wood in forest clearing operations. The coastal hills in the eastern part of the Province between Bluefields and Río Caña are densely settled by Guaymí. And here, as a result of long-continued forest clearing and intermittent regrowth, the johncrow wood population has been greatly increased—even though the trees are eventually cut when they become large enough for making good canoes. At one season this concentration of johncrow wood is especially apparent: the tree blooms in July, at which time the crowns turn yellow with blossoms and stand out sharply. From a boat offshore one can see the flowering crowns sprinkled liberally through regrowth forest along this coastal stretch. But looking farther into hinterland forest, the yellow crowns become increasingly far apart and finally attain the wide spacing characteristic of most tree species there. Thus common forest colors (e.g. lavender *almendro* crowns and yellow johncrow wood) differ from place to place in the Province during the same season—and mostly for cultural reasons.

Chutra is a medium-sized forest tree, the trunks of mature trees being usually three to five feet in diameter. The fruit is green and about the size of a cherry. Though absent on the wet soils of coastal lowlands, it is common in forests farther inland. The Guaymí make various uses of the sap or resin which seeps out of the tree and accumulates in globular masses near the base of the trunk. The product is found in almost every Guaymí household. It has a pleasant piney odor and is burned as incense, and sometimes chewed to freshen the breath. The resin is mixed with the latex of the sambergum and used in caulking boats. Soot from *chutra* resin is also used in making black face paint: Balls of the resin are placed in a hole in the ground a foot or so deep, and set afire. An overturned pot is placed over the hole and the soot collected on its inner surface. The soot is then scraped off and mixed with wax from the axin insect for face paint. But by far the largest amounts of the *chutra* resin are used in the manufacture of carrying bags: the resin is ground to a white powder. Women dip their hands in the powder when rolling thread made from wild pineapple fibers; the powder makes the fibers cling together.

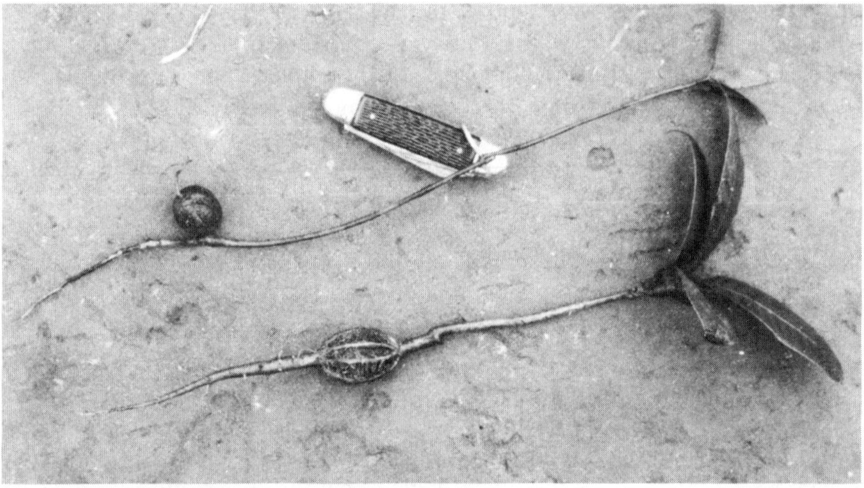

Forest-tree seedlings. The leaves of different species are often confusingly similar; their seeds are less so. A relatively large number of tropical forest trees are large-seeded (Duke, 1969); after sprouting, the seeds of many remain at the ground surface, often clinging to the seedlings for months—thus making ready identification possible. Seedlings of useless plants are easily plucked out (an especially important factor before the introduction of the machete), while useful species are either left growing or transplanted to spots nearer Indian homes. As pathways are extended, and the neighborhood of newly-settled areas is increasingly canvassed for gathered products and game, transformation of the forest begins—seedling selection gradually giving rise to a change in species ratios. Such alteration decreases in intensity with distance from human settlement.

5

GUAYMI AGRICULTURE

Fallowing and Soil Renewal

UNDER NATURAL conditions tropical forests are able to thrive permanently without depleting underlying soils because they are "essentially closed systems, with most of the mineral nutrients being recycled through the system rather than continually obtained from the soil." (Smythe, 1970, p. 31).

On the other hand, a complete clearing of the forest interrupts the cycle and exposes the soil to intensive leaching. Plots which have been clean-cleared and gardened are eventually abandoned because of depletion of their soils in those mineral nutrients required by crop plants. The length of time over which a plot can be profitably gardened depends on several factors, an important one being the number and variety of garden trees included in the plot. Even on fertile streamside soils more then six years of continuous use may not be worthwhile. Thinner soils on hillsides "tire" after only three or four years.

Regrowth vegetation gradually restores mineral nutrients to the soil, perhaps partly because of associated mycorrhizae:

> Recent measurements show that the second growth vegetation can concentrate calcium, phosphorus, nitrogen, and other elements to levels significantly higher (1 percent level) than can nearby climax vegetation on the same soils. (Stark, 1971, p. 229).

How long is regrowth allowed to continue on abandoned plots before they are again cleared and the land re-used? Again, various factors are involved. On floodplains, land may be left only three or four years before it is re-used. On most sites, if regrowth is allowed to continue eight or nine years before clearing, the soils are said to produce almost as well as those from under newly-cleared forest. The period during which land is left fallow under regrowth often depends also upon how badly it is needed; if the land is re-cleared soon, it simply produces less and for a shorter period of time.

Rainforest in hill country generally contains more low-growing plants than does forest growing on flatland because sunlight occasionally penetrates the staggered canopy of forest growing on slopes and stimulates a scattered, mainly woody, undergrowth. Eventually old *rastrojo* re-develops this two-storied character (in places within eight or nine years), and at this time its condition is considered ideal for clearing operations using the machete: then one can easily walk through such old *rastrojo* chopping down the light undergrowth. The slash, allowed to dry, serves as tinder for burning the overgrowing trees. Thus, despite the presence of sizeable trees, old regrowth is thought of as being easier to clear than younger stages because the latter are likely to be a dense growth from top to bottom, hard to penetrate, and wet. (In new regrowth many broad-leaved herbs collect pockets of water in their leaf axils; and in some, e.g. *Costus scaber*, the inflorescence is often almost full of water).

Seeking to preserve useful forest plants, the Guaymí do much less burning of slash than do their Bocatoreño neighbors. Using machetes and axes these days, the Indians are able to cut sizeable tracts of forest down to a height of a meter or so. Fields recently planted to maize are often covered by decaying stumps and branches in such a jumble that it is hard to see the growing maize plants.

Leaving slash unburned may be good agricultural practice. Mineral constituents in the slash are completely released when the organic material is burned. These include plant nutrients which are promptly lost through leaching in this warm and humid climate. Slowly decaying wood, on the other hand, pays the mineral nutrients gradually back into the soil, keeping it fertile for a longer period.

There is little or no tilling of the soil in Guaymí gardens; in planting, a hole is simply made with a twist of the machete blade in the unturned ground, and seeds, seedlings, or cuttings, inserted.

Principal Guaymí maize varieties are especially small-seeded. The seeds are scattered over the ground among the twigs and litter, an unusual way of planting maize. Indeed such broadcasting, as opposed to planting, is generally associated with Old World cereal culture (Sauer, 1952). Before the kernels are sown, they are washed in water in which the leaves of *mata-ratón* have been steeped; this is believed to protect them from rodents. The only maize varieties actually planted, i.e., their seeds dropped into holes in the ground, are large-seeded dent-corns, the types usually grown by non-Indians here.

Crops and Household Animals

THE PRINICIPAL domesticated garden plants (other than trees) grown here in pre-Columbian times were the following: squash, gourd, sweet potato, manioc, wild pineapple (a domesticated variety), ñampi, yautia, pineapple. The chayote, domesticated in Mexico, may have been carried here in the Spanish Colonial period.

Domesticated animals included the: dog, muscovy duck, wax insect, and turkey. The stingless native honeybee was kept in houses.

The following plants and animals were probably introduced here after the arrival of Columbus: banana, rice, dasheen sugar cane, plantain, pig, and chicken.

The most important of the introduced food plants is the banana; it is universally grown at lower elevations. The Guaymí prefer the varieties *conga* and *primitiva* because they require least care, and because they sometimes sprout

Maize-grinding metate in dirt-floored Sabanero-Guaymí house on the upper slope of the Serranía de Tabasará.

A Térraba woman crushing maize. The large stone *mano* is used with a rocking motion. This method, also practiced by the Boruca of Costa Rica (Stone, 1949, p. 8), is not widespread in the Americas. Grinders used with a scrubbing motion (i.e., *metates)* and the pestle used in a mortar with a rotary motion are more common. The mortar in use here is a slab of hardwood; flat stones, somewhat smaller, are also used. The tool is used for crushing various other foodstuffs, in addition to maize.

The muscovy duck; a species domesticated in this general area. The name has nothing to do with Muscovy, being derived instead from *Muisca,* a subdivision of the Chibcha Indians of northwestern Colombia.

spontaneously, growing to maturity from root crowns rather than needing transplanting as do most varieties. (The plantain is generally a more important crop than the banana among tropical tribes, but not so here.) Rice is the only commercial crop, and the pig the principal commercial animal. Another Old World plant, okra, has found its way into many Guaymí gardens, but so far as I know the Indians use it only as a medicine.

Some contend that the Old World plantain and chicken were actually introduced to the Americas, perhaps across the Pacific, in pre-Columbian times (Sauer, 1952).

A domesticated aroid called otó was important in the Caribbean area long before the coming of Europeans; it is also known as yautia. The Guaymí plant a good deal of it. They also cultivate a similar aroid, the dasheen from southeast Asia, which was introduced in post-Columbian times. The two plants can be distinguished readily by their leaves. The dasheen leaf is nearly peltate and light green, wheras the leaf of the otó is sagittate, darker and—particularly the stem—tinged with blue. Both plants have a large central root, used in propagation; and this is the principal edible part of the dasheen. In the otó, however, the main root has a disagreeable spicy flavor. Instead, the small tubers, about the size of sweet potatoes, which grow around it, are eaten; in fact, otó is the root crop preferred here, both by Indians and others. The Guaymí use the leaves of both plants for greens. An advantage of the dasheen over other root crops is that if the tip of the root is cut away; the remainder, if kept dry, can be stored for a long time. The roots of the otó do not keep so long, having a tendency to sprout; yet they keep longer than the roots of the manioc, yam, or sweet potato. The **krunchi** another, very large, aroid is grown by inland Guaymí. All three aroids have the advantage that they are among the last plants to be damaged by leafcutter ants.

Otó (*Xanthosoma nigrum*), an American relative of the Polynesian taro, is cultivated by many tropical American tribes.

The aerial yam is grown by most inland Guaymí and is common among the Térraba too. It has large bulbs, which look something like flattened Irish potatoes, growing in its leaf axils.

Wild pineapple is planted for use in making one of the more characteristic of Guaymí artifacts, their carrying bag. There are two varieties of the wild pineapple: a narrow-leaved form, found wild in the forest, produces a good fiber. The other form, which is cultivated, has broader leaves, and its fiber is superior. Few non-Guaymí are aware that the latter form exists.

Along streams and by water holes near the crest of the Serranía de Tabasará, for instance around Agua Salud, the Guaymí plant a sedge which is used in making hats and the tips for conical roofs. It is grown from cuttings made at the nodes, or from pieces of the roots. I am not sure of the species, but it resembles *Cyperus canus,* a sedge ranging from Guatemala to Colombia, which is described as growing under cultivation in El Salvador (Standley, 1937, p. 97), and among the Mayas: "They have a certain plant which they raise in their wells and in other places, three-cornered like the rush but much thicker, from which they make baskets" (Landa, vol. 18, p. 195; identified as *C. canus* by Lundell).

Other cultivated plants include the turmeric, used for dyeing carrying-bags yellow, and a tall white-flower shrub, *Datura arborea,* grown for medicinal or narcotic uses in the higher parts of Guaymí country. The cultivation of narcotic *Datura* shrubs is known in South America among the southern Chocó Indians—whence this plant perhaps derives—and among several tribes in the upper Amazon.

Near the crest of the Serranía de Tabasará two dooryard trees, the barbados nut and hog plum, are grown by the Guaymí as host plants for axin, a wax-producing scale insect (*Llaveia axin*) once, like its relative the cochineal, important in aboriginal Central America. The same species of insect is cultivated among the Mayas and other Indians in southern Mexico. Since the wild species of the genus *Llaveia* appear to be confined to Guatemala and Mexico, the axin was probably domesticated in that area and carried southeastward into Panama. The insect is raised on the same host trees in both the Guaymí and the Mayan areas and is cared for similarly by the two peoples, the eggs being stored seasonally in dry fiber and corn husks. Furthermore, the wax which the insect produces is extracted, processed, and used in a similar manner in the two areas. Almost certainly, prehistoric connections between the Guaymí and Mexican Indians are involved (Gordon, 1957B).

Beekeeping must once have been a major Indian industry. Honey and wax are repeatedly mentioned as native products traded here to the Spanish in the early 17th century. Bees, a native, stingless species (e.g. *Trigona mosquito frontalis*), are still kept by the Guaymí and Térraba, but only occasionally. The bees grow wild here, often making their nests in termite mounds. They may be brought to the houses, but often take up residence there unaided. Beeswax was once one of the materials used here in making candles and torches. The availability of kerosene as a trade item probably accounts for the decline of an Indian bee industry.

Flower of the **krunchi,** *Xanthosoma,* an aroid cultivated by inland Guaymí. The plant is several times the size of the common coastal otó. Its leaves may rise to a height of 3 meters, with individual leaf blades as much as a meter in length. The swollen rhyzome weighs upward of 7 kg and is edible, though most Guaymí say that dasheen and otó are tastier.

Wild pineapple (locally "wild silk grass" or *pita), Aechmea magdalenae,* is the principal Guaymí fiber plant. The inflorescence which may be 30 cm long has red bracts and encloses small but tasty angular yellow fruits. Actually there are two varieties, distinguished by their leaves: **Kigá mirá,** grows wild; **kigá bogón,** is cultivated.

Tree Gardens

The following are among the trees planted in Guaymí gardens:

achiote
avocado
cacao
calabash tree
coconut (in coastal areas)
conga palm
forest cacao
guagara palms (coastal lowlands only)
guamo del monte
guava
jira palm
jirote palm
mango
membrillo
monkey head
orange
papaya
pataste
peachpalm
rubber tree
sapodilly
tama-tama (coastal gardens)
wild cacao
wild tama-tama (inland gardens)
yellow mombin

Two other trees are said to be planted (I did not find them): one, a balsa-like tree called **krun** ("bark log," in local English) is grown for the fiber in its fruits, used in making pillows; the other *sándi*-like tree, **seguána,** has a drinkable milky latex (*Brosimum utile?*); its bark is used for sleeping mats and poorer grade barkcloth.

Excepting the orange and mango, now present in many gardens, the trees listed are native to the American tropics.

Among the more commonly planted trees are the peachpalm, papaya, *pataste,* monkey head and avocado. These trees are not taken under cultivation directly from local forests, but were rather introduced to the area in the past from other parts of tropical America. They are rarely disseminated by natural means; wherever found, it is likely that they were purposely planted. Although some may survive for a time in regrowth vegetation, they are eventually eliminated in the process of plant succession.

The list will vary from place to place, and it can be greatly extended because, like the forest cacao and rubber tree, various other plants are occasionally carried from surrounding forests for planting near houses; there they are intermixed with garden trees and forest trees left standing from when the clearings were first made.

Monkey head, *Licania platypus,* growing in Guaymí tree garden. Sometimes the fruits are of very irregular shape.

The Guaymí are well aware of the shade requirements of many tree seedlings such as those of forest cacao and *conga* palm. On the other hand, some practices may not be so well founded. For example, they often lodge rocks in the crotches of garden trees, claiming that this keeps flowers and immature fruits from dropping off.

Guaymí and Bókata are the only people in the Province who cultivate the "monkey head" (as it is called by the few English-speakers there who know it). The tree is grown by other Central American tribes, for example the San Blas, and found in parts of a large area between southern Mexico and Colombia. In Bocas del Toro Province few non-Guaymí are familiar with it. The tree has small, white flowers in terminal spikes. The fruit, which is usually somewhat larger than a grapefruit and mottled green, yellow and brown, varies in shape and contains a single, very large, rough seed. (With the coconut, it must be among the largest-seeded plants in Panama.) The thin flesh, which is orange-colored and intermixed with a coarse, woody fiber, has a squash-like odor and tastes rather like candied sweet potato. The main fruiting season appears to be in August and September, but an occasional fruit may mature even in January, at which time the trees are in flower. The plant is apparently not native here: it is not found in neighboring forests and rarely survives where old regrowth covers abandoned gardens.

Although such tree-garden species are often thought of as wild plants simply taken occasionally under cultivation by the Indians, in fact, many are truly domesticated—being unknown as part of an undisturbed flora in those areas where they are cultivated. For example, "The native country of this tree [the monkey head] is somewhat in doubt; Pittier remarks that he has never seen it in a truly wild state" (Woodson and Schery, 1950, vol. 37, p. 172). Possibly the tree derives originally from a point farther east on the Isthmus: On Barro Colorado Island it is described as "Frequent in the forest, especially in old forest." (Croat, 1978, p. 419).

The peachpalm is immensely useful to all Indians in the Province. The fruit is among the three or four most important food sources. The peachpalm is the first tree planted at a new Guaymí homesite; it takes from five to seven years to start bearing fruit. In addition to the fruit, the hearts of suckers which spring up around the tree's base are eaten; although this is a minor food source, it is available when the fruit is green. The Guaymí also crack the roasted seeds (sometimes simply with their teeth) and eat the coconut-flavored kernels; and, for that matter, in times of real scarcity the small, immature fruit itself can be picked and cooked. The tree's hard, dark wood is used for making hunting implements and many other tools. The peachpalm has the great advantage that it is not destroyed by leafcutter ants.

Fruits of the calabash tree are used everywhere among the Indians, as food and drink containers. Every Guaymí, and Toreño, canoe carries a calabash-dipper for bailing; in fact to be at sea without one aboard is considered foolishly unsafe.

The *pataste* is planted over a large part of tropical America, including the Mayan area. Although its "... native region is uncertain ... it is ... in cultivation at least from Chiapas and Tabasco southward to Colombia ... " (Standley and Steyermark, Vol. 6, p. 442); in Colombia, it is cultivated by the Chocó Indians. Actually, its range is even greater than this; Father Cobo described it in Colonial Peru, and it has been noted under cultivation among the Bora and Muinane tribes of northeastern Peru (Tessman, 1930, pp. 271 and 332). *Pataste* is much more important to Indian subsistence in Bocas del Toro Province than is the common cacao, the latter being grown mainly near the coast and for sale.

Pataste occurs here only as a cultivated plant; it is found in virtually every Guaymí, Bókata and Térraba tree garden. Unlike the shade-loving cacao, it is grown in open, sunny spots. In Térraba it is called "wirbu," one of the Spanish commercial names for its seeds; perhaps Térraba is the source of the word.

The corrugated shell of the *pataste* fruit is so hard that it has few pests—the squirrel is about the only tree-climbing animal here that can gnaw through it. The cacao, on the other hand, is eaten by many animals.

Pataste (*Theobroma bicolor*). Note that the small axillary flowers are produced at the same time that fruits are maturing.

The cream-colored flesh of the *pataste* fruit is commonly eaten after the skin is chopped off; the Indians consider it to be more tasty than that of the cacao. The juice is sometimes sucked from the orange flesh of the cacao fruit; otherwise, only its seeds are of use. Since *pataste* seeds contain less oil they do not turn rancid as quickly as do the cacao seeds. The light-colored chocolate which is made from the *pataste* is considered a better drink because when cold it does not have the oily taste of cacao.

The common cacao was also domesticated in Central America, and had spread southward in aboriginal times at least as far as Panama. Although the pre-Columbian distribution of the common cacao is still uncertain, it is probable that the *pataste* was then the more widespread of the two. The Térraba also cultivate a special smooth-fruited variety of the *pataste,* apparently unknown elsewhere.

Wild Cacao (*Herrania purpurea*) is found in regrowth, along forest paths, and planted in Guaymí tree gardens for the acid-sweet pulp surrounding its seeds. Its bark is a Guaymí medicine for scalp infections. The fruits, having ten deep longitudinal corrugations, are covered with short, but prickly, hair and are from five to nine cm long and about four cm thick. About a dozen tetragonal seeds are imbedded in the pulp. The tree is smaller than the *pataste* and has palmate leaves-usually in groups of four and clustered at the top of the tree; it scarcely branches. The fruit, like that of the common cacao, grows along the trunk rather than out on small branchlets, as on the *pataste.*

The *membrillo* (*Gustavia superba;* not to be confused with the several leguminous trees, *Inga* sps., also called "membrillo" here) is a characteristic plant of Indian tree gardens, from western Panama to the Sinú country of Colombia. It is a small tree when fully grown. Saplings are canelike and unbranched, and bear fruit while still quite small. Each fruit contains three of four large spotted seeds. The thick, rough membrane in which these are embedded is eaten cooked in soups or sometimes—despite its leathery texture—raw. Although it is still found in areas of old regrowth where Indian populations have disappeared, little human use is now made of it there, though it is much eaten by monkeys. In Bocas del Toro Province the Guaymí grow the fruit but westward the Térraba seem to be unacquainted with it.

The *membrillo* was one of the more abundant and conspicuous trees cultivated in the Isthmian area when the Spanish arrived and one of the first plants of continental America to be described. Writing in the 16th century, Oviedo gives the following account:

> There is a fruit on the mainland which the Christians call quinces (*membrillos*) though they are not such ... inside the Gulf of Uraba and in many other parts of Cueva [i.e. eastern Panama] ... growing in many thickets, *arcabucos* or forests and abandoned woodlands are a few trees whose fruits look like quinces, because they are of the same size and similarly yellowish; each fruit is round and the size of a big fist ... the skin is cut off with a knife (because it is bitter) and the fruit is cut in quarters, each of which contains an extremely bitter seed which is thrown away; and the remainder of the *membrillo* is thrown in a pot with or without meat ... a good and healthful food. The trees upon which it grows are neither large nor small. It resembles more a sapling than a tree; there are great quantities of these and they bear fruit throughout the larger part of the year. (Oviedo, 1944, Vol. 2, p. 305)

Many of the *arcabucos* (thickets) so frequently referred to by the early Spanish in this area were very likely Indian tree gardens, or patches of tended regrowth.

Thus, tree gardening preserves a rudimentary forest environment in cultivated tracts throughout their years of agricultural use—a major ecological benefit. From the standpoint of Indian subsistence an important effect of such tree gardening is the enrichment of subsequent regrowth vegetation as a source of valuable products: this is true because, on the one hand, those useful trees which are spared when the forest is initially cleared usually survive beyond the years during which the garden tracts are actually tended; and, on the other, because additional useful forest species are carried to the clearings and planted, and these too persist in regrowth for varying periods of time after the gardens are abandoned (as do, in fact, even some of the strictly domesticated trees such as the peachpalm, avocado, etc.).

6

REGROWTH VEGETATION

THE SUCCESSIONAL events associated with partial clearing of tracts of land for agriculture, and reclamation of these sites by regrowth vegetation, roughly resemble those which take place following localized natural disruptions within the forest—for example, following landslides, sudden floods, or the occasional toppling of an aged giant tree. Where bare ground is exposed, its surface is soon covered by spontaneous growth. Most such plant cover is at first low and includes a considerable number of herbaceous species. As time passes the number of woody species increases and eventually the regrowth rises to the height of the original forest. Such secondary cover at any stage, as long as it is readily distinguishable from surrounding forest, is called *rastrojo*, a term much used in this part of Latin America.

A large part of the forest ecosystem has been subjected to cyclic changes of varying duration as a result of periodic human use; most forests in this area are themselves but advanced stages of secondary plant cover, though often not obviously so. Thus, man-induced regrowth is of great ecological importance. On the following pages the *rastrojo* of Guaymí and Bókata country is discussed in some detail.

The regrowth flora of clearings varies with age through complicated successions. Although generalized comment is made here on regrowth characteristics, it should be emphasized that there is actually much variation from place to place, depending partly on local edaphic circumstances and partly upon how and where the clearings were made. For instance, wild cane usually appears on sandy spots near stream banks. Pokeweeds are especially common where the surface of the clearing has been completely burned over. Grass may be the first stage of growth if the clearing is made at the outskirts of the forest near pastures, but not if the clearing is made deep within it.

In younger *rastrojo,* where only a year or two has passed since the original clearing was made, the *Scitaminae,* especially species of *Heliconia,* usually form a good deal of the plant cover. In tracts of older *rastrojo* where several years or more have passed since the original clearing was abandoned, tree growth will have developed, the amount of shade has increased, and the heliophile *Scitaminae* are less plentiful. In coastal areas small regrowth trees may include *oreja de mula* which comes up only on swampy ground, or *nance de montaña* (*Byrsonima*, probably a new species; Dr. Thomas B. Croat, personal communication) which, though found on sloping stream banks, avoids swampy sites. In the later stages of succession the regrowth takes on the appearance of surrounding forest—adjusting in its species content to the local physiographic and edaphic setting, whether it be ridge, slope, floodplain or swamp.

Looking southward up a small tributary of the Rio Calovébora. This vegetation is largely regrowth as a result of the agricultural practices of the Bókata Indians.

Guarumo (*Cecropia* sp.) No other tree is more characteristic of regrowth vegetation in tropical American forests. The trunk and branches are smooth, light-colored, ringed and hollow. The flowers are borne in finger-like catkins enclosed, while immature, in a sheath. Note the cluster of catkins exposed after the sheath has fallen away. The tiny seeds are dispersed by fruit-eating birds. Sloths and monkeys browse on the leaves.

USEFUL REGROWTH PLANTS

UNDER INDIAN LAND use here, regrowth vegetation provides many useful products and a considerable food supply. This is true in other parts of these tropics as well; for example, in the artificial savannas of the Colombian Sinú country Indian communities, though now surrounded by pastures of alien grasses, still maintain patches of regrowth and collect there some of the same species used by the Guaymí.

1. Garden Weeds and Plants of First Regrowth

As Guaymí gardens are abandoned and crop plants die, garden weeds become dominant in the first stage of regrowth; actually many of these are valuable, and "weeds" only in the sense that they are not planted and sometimes cut down to make room for crops. Plants of the garden and the first stage of regrowth provide most of the Guaymí's starchy foods. In addition to common crop plants the following are the principal sources:

regrowth-yam	*Dioscorea standleyi*
wild sweet potato	*Ipomea acuminata*

A purple-flowered vine, very like a morning glory. The edible tubers are white and sweet. The plant is generally found at elevations of over a thousand feet.

panama hat plant	*Carludovica palmata*

The panama hat plant is typical regrowth throughout much of the American tropics. The immature inflorescence, a cylindrical spadix enclosed in a husk of soft spathes, looks something like an ear of corn; it is roasted and its interior eaten. As the plant often grows in sizeable clumps or large beds, and may flower heavily, it has the advantage of yielding food in quantity. The Guaymí refer to it as an emergency subsistence resource; and the plant figures in their stories of tribal creation. Nevertheless, it is by no means considered a choice food, but rather something always available in case of need. Where the panama hat plant is absent in clearings the Guaymí sometimes plant it, using either cuttings from its roots, or seeds—as do descendants of the Zenú tribe in Colombia. The leaves have a variety of uses among Central and South American Indians, including use as thatch, make-shift umbrellas, etc. More important to commerce, it was the basis in Ecuador of the so-called panama-hat industry which flourished in the early part of this century.

In addition to these sources of starch, crop plants such as *ñampi* and aerial yam continue to come up in regrowth for a year or two after clearings are abandoned; and the Guaymí occasionally gather their tubers.

The following are some of the plants which the Guaymí eat for greens; garden weeds and plants of new regrowth are their principal source:

do-mi	*Pachyptera standleyi*	Bignoniaceae
garden fern	*Ctenitis sloanei*	Polypodiaceae

Panama-hat plant, *Carludovica sp.;* cattle ranch on the lower Río Teribe in the background.

Regrowth-yam, *Dioscorea standleyi*? The undersides of the leaves are purple. The vine grows in Guaymí gardens and new *rastrojo,* where it is often treated as a weed; but in clearings where it is absent, it may be planted. Regrowth yam is a basic subsistence food in that the Guaymí fall back upon its tubers in bad times when little other starchy food is available. According to Guaymí creation myths, the regrowth-yam and the panama-hat plant were the first food plants put on the earth with the Indian.

Although fern tips are occasionally eaten in many parts of the world, among the Indians of Bocas del Toro Province they are a major food item—probably because this edible species comes up so copiously in all gardens. Five or six inches of the fern's growing tip are broken off and boiled. The cooked tips look and taste something like thin green asparagus shoots. Before leaving the fields for home in the evening, women commonly collect the tips, tying them together in small bundles. Boiled fern tips and peachpalm fruit are a traditional meal for all tribes in the Province; among the Guaymí great quantities of the fern are eaten at feasts celebrating births.

kigia	*Malachra* sp.	Malvaceae
ñenge	*Urera baccifera*	Urticaceae
ñériga	*Elateriopsis oerstedii*	Cucurbitaceae
nu-sula	*Melothria dulcis*	Cucurbitaceae
pokeweed	*Phytolacca rivinoides*	Phytolaccaceae

Of the seven species listed above, all except the **do-mi** may be garden weeds, and all are common in regrowth less than two years old. Only the young leaves of the **kigia** and **ñenge** are picked, their petioles and stems being covered with irritant prickles.

In older *rastrojo* there are fewer of such greens-plants: the **do-mi** is one, though to be sure its leaves are thin with little soft tissue. Greens are scarce in mature forest.

mazó *Witheringia solanacea*
An inland species, covered in July with small orange berries.

nulia *Cestrum* sp.
An inland species, bearing both flowers and tiny white berries in July.

The following plants bear edible fruits:

wild papaya *Carica cauliflora* ?
A small, unbranched tree; its orange fruits grow directly from the trunk.

square-stemmed passion flower *Passiflora quadrangularis*
This vine bears large, bright-green fruits.

Good fish-poisoning plants are rare in regrowth; two which are said to yield at least poor quality poisons are the following nightshade family shrubs:

Nériga, *Elateriopsis oerstedii,* a squash-like vine; its leaves are eaten as greens.

The following statement about the square-stemmed passion flower suggests how difficult it is to trace the derivation of various growth species: "Widely cultivated and escaping throughout tropical America—of uncertain origin" (Woodson and Sherry, 1958, vol. 45, p. 18).

Several garden weeds are used in making tea; for example, a small shrubby melastome, *Arthrostemma ciliatum.* The *culantro,* found as a weed in coastal clearings, is planted in inland gardens for use as a spice on boiled meat.

Of great use everywhere as wrapping and rain-shedding material are the leaves characteristic of new-growth plants—and this despite increasing importation, and the careful saving, of plastic wrappings by the Indians. Most used of all are the leaves of *bijaos:* these include plants of the banana family—especially the genus *Heliconia*—and the arrowroot family, e.g. the genus *Calathea.*

Cowfoot, or *juanico, Piper auritum,* in coastal regrowth, has a pleasant mintlike aroma. The genus *Piper* is well-represented here among garden weeds and plants of new regrowth.

2. Older Regrowth

Within two or three years most of the low-growing large-leaved herbs which are so common in newer *rastrojo* will have become scarce. On the other hand, very tall herbs such as beafsteak heliconia which forms dense thickets, may survive several years in regrowth. (Beafsteak heliconia, unlike most *bijaos,* is of little use; its leaves split and cannot be used as wrapping material). Shrubs and small trees then become the principal plant cover. In some tracts of two-year-old regrowth saplings may rise to a height of 5 m to 8 m, and be 5 cm to 8 cm in diameter.

Red inflorescence and leaves of *Costus,* a genus of ginger family herbs at forest edges, along trails, and in regrowth vegetation in clearings.

A *bijao, Heliconia pogonatha* (banana family) which, like the beefsteak heliconia, forms dense cover in new regrowth. The leaves are used for food wrappers, makeshift umbrellas, grave linings, etc. In the centers of its red fruit-clusters are tiny, pale, bananalike fruits which are eaten by the Guaymí and Térraba, as are the white centers of new leaf shoots.

Below are listed some plants, useful to the Guaymí, which are present in *rastrojo,* which is two to five years old:

balsa — *Ochroma pyramidale*
The tree is widely known for its light wood. Its saplings and those of other trees of the silk-cotton family are cut for use as casting sticks at *balserias.*

bribri — *Inga minutula*
A very productive small or medium-sized tree: people, squirrels, parrots, etc. eat the sweet pulp which envelops seeds in its small spiraling pods.

cocoita
Wood burns when freshly cut (true of few other *rastrojo* trees). Its fruits are much eaten by toucans, agoutis, squirrels, etc. Especially common near forest edges.

chica — *Arrabidaea chica*
This plant was once of great importance in aboriginal America, although it is scarcely known to non-Indians. It is associated with wooded areas, being a liana. The species ranges all the way from Mexico to Argentina and is found in a great variety of terrains. The Guaymí plant the *chica* in shady spots and use its leaves to make an purple dye for coloring carrying bags. Though hard to recognize, the plant is not uncommon in regrowth and secondary forest, e.g. along the Río San Pedrito. The Maya also use *chica* for dyeing (Seibert, 1940, p. 404) as do the Cuna Indians of eastern Panama, and various Amazonian tribes of the Río Meta on the east side of the Andes. In Colombia descendants of the Zenú tribe still cultivate it in their tree gardens and prepare from it a black dye for basketry and hats, by a fermenting process. Preparing dyes by boiling and fermenting the plant's leaves was widespread (Lévi-Strauss, 1950, p. 478). That the plant's distribution is associated with Indian populations is well known. In parts of its range its occurrence is "the certain indication of the site of an old aboriginal settlement, destroyed after the conquest." (Vezga, 1936, Vol. 47, p. 147)

carachero — *Vismia macrophylla*
A small tree with red flaky bark; common in coastal lowlands. The wood is much used for house frames.

guamo del monte — *Inga* sp.
The sweet pulp around the seeds is edible. It attracts many animals too.

kongi — *Mucuna* sp.
A leguminous vine, bearing large rectangular, paired seed pods. The leaves are steeped in water to make a black dye used on carrying bags.

kógru — *Cissus microcarpa*
This plant is of no subsistence value, but nevertheless of great importance to the Guaymí. It also grows on streambanks, usually as a trailing vine. In *rastrojo* on the other hand it could often more appropriately be called a liana, since its stems become thick and woody; they nevertheless remain surprisingly pliant, almost rubbery, and are used to fence out devils or evil spirits. The spirits are exorcised from a troubled household by a *sukia;* then wild cane and *guarumo* stakes are driven into the ground in a circle around the house, and segments of **kógru** stem interwoven through the stakes. Such fences are said to exclude evil. Another regrowth liana, *Cordia spinescens,* is also used in spiritual rituals.

monkey apple — *Posoqueria latifolia*

Monkey apple *Posoqueria latifolia,* a small or medium sized tree of the madder family. The globular fruit, about 4 cm in diameter, is a minor human food item, but is of greater attraction to birds and other animals. The seeds are enveloped in a sweet, yellow pulp. (The fruit in the photograph has been partly eaten by parrots). The leaves look much like over-sized coffee leaves, and, in fact, the tree is often called "wild coffee." Although typical of rocky shoreline and headlands, the monkey apple also spreads to regrowth some distance inland. The photograph was taken at shoreline; note the sea-fan coral (*Gorgonia*) in the background.

Oreja de mula (*Bellucia axinanthera*) a tall shrub of the melastome family, common in old lowland regrowth. There, the plant is one of the most important sources of animal food because it bears fruit in large quantity throughout much of the year. The fruit is eaten by birds, peccaries, feral hogs, etc. The leaves, steeped in water, produce black dye for carrying bags.

nance — *Byrsonima crassifolia*
A small tree with edible yellow fruit. The *nance* is especially common on the Pacific side of the Isthmus. Here it is found mainly near the coast.

oreja de mula — *Bellucia axinanthera*

pigeon plum — *Hirtella latifolia*
A small tree with edible yellow fruit.

polewood — *Guatteria aeruginosa* and *G. lucens*
Small to medium-sized trees with straight trunks. Very common in older coastal regrowth. Their wood is much used in making house fences and piling.

reedwater tree — *Simara maxonii*
A small tree with very large leaves and sprays of brilliant yellow flowers in its crown. It is often left standing near Indian houses for ornament. It is used in making a red dye.

rubber tree — *Castilla elastica*
At one time both Indians and Toreños sought out the rubber tree and tapped it. But there is no longer a commercial demand for rubber made from its latex. Coagulated and sun-dried, the latex turns black; hence Toreños call the tree *caucho negro* to distinguish its rubber from that of the sapodilly. Guaymí sometimes plant the tree which perhaps accounts for the fact that it is more commonly found in *rastrojo* than in mature forest.

wild lime *Xylosma* sp.
Tall coastal shrub with blue berry-like fruit used in dyeing carrying bags.

zobágria *Maripa nicaraguensis*
Liana often found draped over small tree in inland *rastrojo.* The yellow fruit contains a syrupy edible fluid; the plant is similar to the forest species, *Maripa panamensis,* mentioned earlier.

In addition to the above species, surviving garden trees such as *jira*-palm, *membrillo,* and wild cacao, are scattered through some tracts of regrowth; the products of these trees are occasionally harvested, too.

WITHIN FIVE YEARS the dominance of regrowth by shrubs is broken, and crowns of medium-sized trees cover most of the surface. Regrowth in these last stages is richer in species, despite the fact that most of the *rastrojo* plants listed above have become considerably less common, or disappeared. The regrowth begins to take on structural characteristics of the surrounding forest: Shade tolerant shrubs remain, but they are more scattered. (One can walk about more easily here than in younger regrowth.) A few undergrowth palms appear. Vines are replaced by lianas, a particularly large species being the sea bean. Parasitic shrubs, such as *mato palo* of the mistletoe family, occasionally grow on tree branches—as does an epiphytic bromeliad, *Tillandsia bulbosa.* Regrowth in these later stages can often be recognized both because it still has not reached the height of the surrounding forest, and because within it certain species persist in concentrated stands. For example, in places *cigarillo* and polewood, having overtopped tall shrubs, are still plentiful. Other trees, such as *cocito de mono* and *almácigo,* whose saplings were inconspicuous in younger regrowth, may become dominant trees in some tracts at lower elevations. (*Almácigo* is well known in the many parts of Central America where it is used as living fence; its branches, stuck in the soil, take root quickly. The tree is easily recognized by its smooth bark which peels in thin, irregular sheets—green sheets on young trees and red on older specimens.) But most such concentrations are broken up by the time tree heights and diameters equal those found in surrounding mature forest.

Cocito de mono, Guarea multiflora, a tree found commonly in some advanced regrowth, and occasionally in the forest. (The fruit is almost mature in January, as shown here.)

Origins and Dissemination of Rastrojo Vegetation

A NUMBER OF SPECIES common in the early stages of regrowth can also be found scattered thinly through neighboring forest. Of forest species whose seeds germinate in the soil of newly formed clearings, many are heliophiles favored by the increase in available light. But most regrowth species are disseminated not from forest to clearing but from one clearing to another.

The following are a few of the many forest plants which become more numerous in abandoned clearings:

Aphelandra crenata	Acanthaceae
Heliconia latispatha	Musaceae
Pentagonia macrophylla	Rubiaceae
Psychotria polyphlebia	Rubiaceae
Thecophyllum insigne	Bromeliaceae
Vismia angusta	Guttiferae

Probably a large part of the regrowth flora derives originally from the banks of streams, with a few additional species coming from the coastal shoreline: The plant cover of streambanks contains a larger proportion of heliophiles than does the forest proper. Furthermore, such vegetation is well-adapted to frequent natural disturbance by flooding, and thus withstands better than other forest plants the artificial disturbances associated with man-made clearings. The riparian origin of old-field vegetation has been pointed out elsewhere (Allen, 1956, p. 69).

Some of the plant species which spread from streamsides to become part of the regrowth in clearings are the following:

Byrsonima spec. nov. ?	Malphighiaceae
Carludovica palmata	Cyclanthaceae
Cissus microcarpa	Vitaceae
Melothria dulcis	Cucurbitaceae
Mucuna sp.	Leguminosae
Paragonia pyramidata	Bignoniaceae
Tovomita sp.	Guttiferae
Passiflora auriculata	Passifloraceae

Thus, in areas where people are absent the panama-hat plant grows mainly in small patches at streamside, but in inhabited areas it is widespread in abandoned clearings; the same is true of many other plants.

Several plants which grow naturally near the coastal shoreline also range short distances inland to become regrowth when old fields there are abandoned; for example, the following small or medium-sized trees. The *nance* and *nancillo,* from the inland edges of barrier beaches; the monkey apple, from rough coastal headlands; and a tree of the myrtle family (a species of *Marlierea* ?), spreading from the banks of coastal *caños,* where it grows with the wild soursop.

On the other hand, many regrowth species have been disseminated so widely by birds from one ancient man-made clearing to another that their places of origin may be distant indeed from the *rastrojo* in which they now grow.

Only a few alien plants have been naturalized here. Such species occasionally appear, or are planted, in disturbed spots (gardens, pastures, etc.); but they are soon eliminated in the successional process.

Almost no foreign species penetrate and establish themselves in mature plant associations. The tropical almond, a native of Asia, is an exception, but even it is restricted to the vicinity of shoreline where vegetation is constantly disturbed (albeit in this case naturally) by tides and waves. The tree grows to a height of some thirty meters. The ripening fruit is fleshy, red on one side and green on the other, and contains an almond-like seed. When the tree was brought here is unknown, but its introduction has had various ecological effects; several native animals, e.g. squirrels and crabs, have taken to eating its fruit (actually most of the fruit lies beneath the trees uneaten for long periods). Littoral drift is apparently important in its spread: germinating seeds and seedlings can be found in the swash along much of the coast.

Seasonality in Garden and Regrowth

LOCAL TERMS for describing climatic seasons are vague. For instance, along the coast when speaking of a season of bad weather, Toreños are simply referring to a period of heavy seas. A certain amount of rainfall is taken for granted at any time of the year.

Among the Guaymí themselves progression of the seasons is associated mainly with sequent biotic change. Asked, for example, when a particular fruit ripens, a Guaymí is likely to answer that it does so, say, just before or after something else bears fruit or flowers; certainly he can rarely name the month if he speaks Spanish. Few Guaymí have acquired printed calendars or knowledge of their use—although government schools and church missions are changing this. (For reckoning the time of an upcoming event—as in the case of a stick game—a given number of knots are tied in strings which are then distributed to those who plan to participate. A knot is cut off the string each day, the agreed-upon date arriving when all knots are gone). Although phases of the moon are important to both Guaymí and Bocatoreño in deciding crop planting time, the former apparently make no connection between lunar phases and a calendar of the sun.

The following are a few Guaymí seasons: "when the wild cane flowers" (June): "turtle time" (around July); "when the *tití* fish run" (most strongly in August); "the big peachpalm harvest" (October); "beachward migration of the iguana and white land crab" (mainly in April); and, farther inland, "when the curassow cries"—generally around May. (During its breeding season the great curassow's cries resound through the forest—an alarming and unbirdlike roaring better suited to a sizeable carnivore).

Developmental changes for most wild species are prompted by periodic changes in physical environment—the so-called "cosmo-rhythms" which are mainly the consequence of the changing position of the sun. Tree species growing in undisturbed portions of the forest usually have seasons of development which are definite enough that they can be anticipated month by month. And in Bocas del Toro Province numerous species flower or fruit in each month of the year. Presumably most such developmental changes are directly elicited by fluctuations in temperature and rainfall (even though amplitudes are small) or by variations in light.

Dry season and time of flowering are associated in other parts of Panama, in Chiriquí Province for example. Similarly in the Canal Zone, at Barro Colorado Island, "The number of species of large and medium-sized trees in flower increases with the onset of the dry season [and] reaches a peak in February ... the onset of the dry season acts to synchronize flowering of a large percentage of the island's flora" (Croat, 1969, p. 300).

Conditions are different in Bocas del Toro Province: although there are usually two yearly reductions in the amount of rainfall, these can hardly be described as dry seasons—since their intensity and monthly incidence are not consistent from year to year; and since in occasional years such periods of reduced rainfall do not occur at all. No particularly large number of plants flower or fruit at these times.

Most wild plants have their own characteristic reproductive seasons, but the majority appear to be independent of rainfall fluctuations. Along the coast the seagrape has one flowering season in late December and early January—at which time the trees also carry a crop of immature fruit; this is one of the rainiest times of the year. (Apparently the tree has yet another flowering, the time of which I am uncertain). Fruit ripens in March and again in September-October, the latter being the larger crop. Thus, in the seagrape's case it is fruit-ripening, rather than flowering, that corresponds best with the drier seasons.

Plainly periodic changes in plant cover are less synchronous and definite here than in most other climates. On Pacific slopes of the Isthmus not only flowering but other physiologic changes are in phase with climatic seasons, for example a number of species are deciduous during the dry months. But here in the mainly evergreen forests of the Atlantic slopes, several large trees either follow an inner ancestral rhythm established in another clime or respond to an environmental control which is not apparent: the *laurel* almost completely sheds its leaves in July-August, as does the milk tree in May, and the yellow mombin and monkey comb in January—despite heavy rains. Furthermore, there are some plants in which the inner rhythm has a weak and uncertain beat; Schimper many years ago (1903, p. 245) observed that "In all tropical districts with weak climatic periodicity there are woody plants that shed their leaves at longer or shorter intervals (one to six times a year) without any connection with the season of the year ... trees of one and the same species ... in other cases individual twigs shed their leaves and acquire fresh ones at different times."

There is another way in which weakened association between developmental changes in plants and periodic changes in physical environment manifests itself. Instead of having an uncertain and varying rhythm of development as described by Schimper, the plant maintains its characteristic developmental tempo but is capable of starting its cycle at any time of the year. Thus the plant's cycle of development has been "detached," so to speak, from climatic and other cosmorhythmic cycles. This characteristic, which can be noted especially in plants of the regrowth, appears to be a trend in the process of domestication, since it is even more pronounced in domesticated species. The flowering seasons of several regrowth plants (for instance, wild papaya, species of *Costus,* and pokeweed) appear to date from the time at which the clearing was made, a characteristic rendering such plants especially useful as they can be made to grow at the times when they are most wanted. For example, pokeweed comes up so predictably immediately after fires that inland Térraba reburn small patches in older regrowth to produce the plant on an almost crop-like basis for use as edible greens. Such flexibility can be used to great advantage in arranging the seasonal development of vegetation suitable to human needs. The breaking of cosmorhythmic links appears to be one effect of disturbing the natural forest.

As noted above, concentrations of a single species are rare in undisturbed forest, except on edaphically distinctive sites like swampland. Thus the almost pure stands which often occur in regrowth are of special genetic interest. The number of individuals of a particular species is much greater per unit area here than in undisturbed vegetation. Because of their numerical preponderance, and hence the greater abundance of pollen produced, these plants are likely to feed the genes of physiological mutants back strongly to congeners scattered throughout the surrounding forest, thus transmitting to wild populations those traits which make for successful growth in clearings.

Among some anciently domesticated species, a former synchrony of developmental changes in the plant with rhythmic changes of the physical environment seems to have been weakened or broken; periodicity in such plants now appears to be dictated by an independent inner rhythm. For example, maize and rice harvests can be dated, with only small variations, from the time of planting; most varieties taking a little over four months to mature. Thus, although life span and developmental sequence in these plants is definite according to species, the time of initiating the life cycle can be chosen by the agriculturist regardless of such periodic factors as the changing position of the sun.

Otó, manioc, dasheen, plantain, banana, sugar cane, etc., all vegetatively reproduced, can be planted at any time. (The fact that the banana can be planted in any month and harvested after a predictable maturation period, means that its fruit can be made available the year around; for this reason it is both an ideal subsistence and commercial crop.) But even among vegetatively reproduced plants seasonal expressions may remain. The pineapple ripens most of its fruit here in June. And, although ñampi roots can be harvested over a long period, they are of best quality in December.

Phenological information is unfortunately confused and scanty for most of the Isthmian area, no comprehensive account having been given of the flowering seasons of wild and regrowth plants, nor even of the harvest seasons of the cultivated ones. (See, however, Croat, 1969 and 1978).

1. Flowering and Fruiting Time in Tree Gardens

THERE ARE TWO main harvests of peachpalm during the year: a heavy harvest in September-October, and a smaller one in February-March. On the other hand, in the westernmost part of the Province quantities of fruit are already being harvested in August. Furthermore, an occasional tree ripens its fruit in an off-season, and one may find a few ripe fruits even in January or June. Then too, in time of need immature fruit is sometimes cooked and eaten.

Similarly, the main commercial harvest of cacao is in September-October, with another season of somewhat decreased yield, called *postrera* in February-March; but again, some cacao fruit ripens throughout the year, though more nuts fall in some months than others. The *pataste* also ripens over a long period; for example, in August the trees are simultaneously bearing flowers and nearly ripened fruit. On the other hand, the wild cacao appears to have a single, rather definite season: it flowers in January and bears mature fruit in July-August.

The monkeyhead bears fruit sporadically. May is said to be its principal month, but just as harvest times for certain species vary from place to place in the Province, so may they vary from year to year. In June of 1978 I was unable to find trees bearing fruit; in June of 1979 I found a considerable number doing so. Occasionally ripe fruit appears on the trees in January, at which time the tree usually flowers heavily.

Oviedo long ago noted that the *membrillo* bears fruit throughout much of the year; for instance, in January one can find flowers, small immature fruits, and ripening fruit simultaneously present on a single branch. And the tree calabash, native to Central America ... "flowers irregularly throughout the year" (Gentry, 1973, vol. 60, p. 832). The papaya also bears continuously, the fruits ripening one by one; a few trees planted around a home will supply fresh fruit throughout the year. Thus, the tree garden as a whole is continuously productive, with no single harvest season.

2. Seasonality in Rastrojo Plants

Rastrojo Plants Collected (Late December to Mid-January 1975, 1978)
(fl. = flowering; fr. = bearing fruit ; fl. & fr. = simultaneously flowering and bearing fruit)

Aphelandra crenata	Acanthaceae	fl.
Bellucia axinanthera	Melastomaceae	fl. & fr.
Byrsonima crassifolia	Malpighiaceae	fr.
Calea prunifolia	Compositae	fl.
Carica cauliflora ?	Moraceae	fl.
Cecropia sp.	Moraceae	fr.
Centropogon sp.	Campanulaceae	fl.
Cephaelis elata	Rubiaceae	fr.
Cephaelis tomentosa	Rubiaceae	fl. & fr.
Cissus microcarpa	Vitaceae	fl.
Compelia zanonia	Commelinaceae	fl. & fr.
Conostegia xalapensis	Melastomaceae	fl. & fr.
Cordia spinescens	Boraginaceae	fl. & fr.
Cytharexylum crassifolia	Verbenaceae	fr.
Dioclea wilsonii	Leguminosae	fl.
Faramea sp.	Rubiaceae	fr.
Gouania lupuloides	Rhamnaceae	fl.
Guarea multiflora ?	Meliaceae	fr.
Guatteria aeruginosa	Annonaceae	fl. & fr.
Inga minutula	Leguminosae	fl.
Inga pezizifera	Leguminosae	fl. & fr.
Isertia haenkeana	Rubiaceae	fr.
Lantana sp.	Verbenaceae	fl. & fr.
Melanthera aspera	Compositae	fl.
Miconia nutans ?	Melastomaceae	fr.
Miconia simplex	Melastomaceae	fl.
Oryctanthus cordifolius	Loranthaceae	fl. & fr.
Phytolacca rivinoides	Phytolaccaceae	fl. & fr.
Piper auritum	Piperaceae	fl. & fr.
Posoqueria latifolia	Rubiaceae	fl. & fr.
Simara maxonii	Rubiaceae	fr.
Siparuna pauciflora	Monimiaceae	fl.
Xylosma sp.	Flacourtiaceae	fl.

Rastrojo Plants Collected, (mid-June to mid-July 1978-1979)

(fl. = flowering; fr. = bearing fruit; fl. & fr. = simultaneously flowering and bearing fruit)

Aphelandra crenata	Acanthaceae	fl.
Arthostema ciliatum	Melastomaceae	fl.
Bellucia axinanthera	Meliaceae	fl. & fr.
Callicarpa acuminata	Verbenaceae	fl. & fr.
Cassipourea elliptica	Rhizophoraceae	fr.
Carica cauliflora ?	Caricaceae	fl. & fr.
Cecropia sp.	Moraceae	fr.
Cephaelis elata	Rubiaceae	fl.
Cephaelis tomentosa	Rubiaceae	fl. & fr.
Cestrum sp.	Solanaceae	fl. & fr.
Clibadium grandifolium	Compositae	fl.
Clidemia septuplinervia	Melastomaceae	fl. & fr.
Compsoneura sprucei	Myristicaceae	fr.
Cordia dwyeri	Boraginaceae	fr.
Cornutia grandifolia	Verbenaceae	fl.
Costus scaber	Zingiberaceae	fr.
Guatteria aeruginosa	Annonaceae	fl.
Guatteria lucens	Annonaceae	fl.
Heisteria longipes	Olacaceae	fr.
Inga minutula	Leguminosae	fr.
Isertia hypoleuca	Rubiaceae	fl. & fr.
Justicia glabra	Acanthaceae	fl.
Lantana sp.	Verbenaceae	fl. & fr.
Ludwigia octovalvis	Onagraceae	fl.
Maripa nicaraguensis	Convolvulaceae	fr.
Marlierea sp.	Myrtaceae	fr.
Melothria dulcis	Cucurbitaceae	fr.
Miconia dolichorrhyncha	Melastomaceae	fr.
Miconia lonchophylla	Melastomaceae	fl.
Miconia prasina	Melastomaceae	fl.
Neea amplifolia	Nyctaginaceae	fr.
Paragonia pyramidata	Bignoniaceae	fr.
Passiflora tryphostemmatoides	Passifloraceae	fl. & fr.
Pentagonia macrophylla	Rubiaceae	fl.
Phytolacca rivinoides	Phytolaccaceae	fl. & fr.
Piper auritum	Piperaceae	fl. & fr.
Posoqueria latifolia	Rubiaceae	fr.
Psychotria polyphlebia	Rubiaceae	fr.
Psychotria racemosa	Rubiaceae	fr.
Psychotria suerrensis	Rubiaceae	fl.
Simara maxonii	Rubiaceae	fl.
Siparuna pauciflora	Monimiaceae	fr.
Tococa guianensis	Melastomaceae	fl. & fr.
Tovomita sp.	Guttiferae	fr.
Vismia macrophylla	Guttiferae	fl. & fr.

The table shows that the regrowth flora as a whole quite definitely has no synchronous flowering or fruit-bearing season, or seasons. In both January and July regrowth plants can be divided into three groups in almost equal numbers: plants flowering, plants bearing fruit, and plants simultaneously flowering and bearing fruit; perhaps a slightly higher proportion of plants bear fruit in July than in January. Almost one third of all species in the list can be found with both flowers and fruit in one or the other of these two months; and several bear both flowers and fruit in both months, i.e. probably almost continuously throughout the year. There seems to be little relationship between these reproductive events and periods of reduced or increased rainfall.

The *cigarillo* can be taken as an example of those regrowth trees with a single, fairly definite fruiting season. The tree, which often forms small, nearly pure stands, is a fast-growing species; it may rise to a height of over 10 m in three-to-five-year-old *rastrojo*, with trunks 15 to 25 cm. in diameter. In January, the *cigarillo* flowers profusely, and the trees can be seen as lavender patches in hillside regrowth. (On the Pacific side of Central America the tree flowers in March and April—Allen, 1957, p. 236.) In July the tree bears a large crop of its flat, rectangular seed pods, but even at this time one can find a few flowers.

At shoreline the tropical almond, an introduced Asian tree, flowers heavily in July, producing spikes of small, pale-yellow flowers; at that time, it bears no fruit at all—immature or ripe. In January it flowers again, but at the same time bears a crop of full-size, almost ripened fruit. In May and early June a crop of ripe fruit litters the ground. Thus, there are at least two flowering and fruiting seasons in the year. While comparison of the tropical almond with other exotic trees shows some correspondence in their reproductive seasons, it mainly illustrates again the indecisive seasonal effects of local climate. The mango, another native of tropical Asia, fruits once—at roughly the same time that the tropical almond is bearing one of its crops, i.e. in May and early June. On the other hand, the rose apple, a native of the Pacific islands, produces a single heavy crop in January, although a few fruits can be found ripening throughout the year.

3. Seasonality in Rastrojo Animals

THE FACT THAT all extensive tracts of regrowth here are the result of human activity means that human custom has become an important factor in the evolution of animal life. Indian inhabitants having modified plant cover within tropical American forests for millenia, have, at the same time, changed animal habits, numbers, and distributions.

Seasonality appears to be less characteristic of regrowth plants than of species growing in the forest. As indicated in the above lists, some regrowth plants produce fruit almost throughout the year; thus, various animals are attracted to regrowth because their principal foods are produced there in a sustained supply. Furthermore production of animal foods is augmented on regrowth sites. Whereas scattered distribution is characteristic of forest plants, in regrowth the species number is reduced and individuals of the same kind often grow close together; this makes for concentration of animal food supply. Regrowth, particularly in its early stages, provides unusually large amounts of soft leafy food for herbivores. In intermediate stages of regrowth, food becomes especially plentiful for fruit-eating animals—because of the abundance of shrubs bearing fleshy fruits and berries.

That various animals adjust their seasons of reproduction to those of the vegetation upon which they depend is indicated in the following notes: "... in Central America birds can reproduce at any period of the year, so long as conditions are favorable for rearing their offspring. Of these conditions, abundance of food appears to be the most important." (Skutch, 1950, p. 211). And another study made in Panama, found that "... frugivorous birds synchronize their breeding cycles with the period of maximum fruit abundance." (Leck, 1970, p. 583). Thus, regrowth and garden vegetation in Bocas del Toro Province, being comparatively seasonless, tend to eliminate season in birds, as well. For example, nests of the little tinamu, a characteristic *rastrojo* species, can be found virtually throughout the year.

Based upon his observations in nearby Costa Rica, a well-known naturalist implies that landuse practices may be important in the evolution of animal life. For birds "... of the second growth thickets, in particular, the proper adjustments of their breeding season to the agricultural practices of man would have survival value." (Skutch, 1950, p. 215).

In contrast to much of Central America where clearing is done at a definite dry season, here in Bocas del Toro clearing is done sporadically throughout the year, so that all stages of regrowth and all variety of habitat can be found at any given time within a small area.

In terms of Guaymí subsistence, regrowth and garden vegetation not only makes certain game animals available in larger numbers than in undisturbed forest, but insures their availability throughout the year.

Further on the subject of human influences upon seasonal development—the felling of trees and slashing of plants with the machete, itself somewhat alters seasonal development. Such pruning delays or stimulates flowering in some species. All along the shoreline, e.g. in Bocas itself, the margarita, a low-growing, yellow-flowered composite comes up and flowers quickly after *macheteros* chop it back—at whatever time of year that may be. *Mata-ratón* planted in fence rows and pollarded, does not flower at its usual season—January. Normally, the *kurutú* is leafless in January; but at that very time, a profusion of leaves sprout from *kurutú* stumps in forest clearings.

Because the populations, ranges and seasonal developments of dozens of interacting plant and animal species vary according to the history of human land use, ecological discussions of Panamanian forests which do not take former human presence and custom into account are incomplete—the ecosystem as a whole being constantly in a state of adjustment to human inteference. Thus, to be realistic, ecological models of the rainforest usually require inclusion of an anthropogenic factor, though the requirement is rarely taken seriously. (It is this significant human social factor, by the way, which precludes total integration of ecology into the "natural sciences".) At times, the evolutionary effects of the anthropogenic factor have been creative, rather than destructive. In any case its expressions can be read on a grand scale in regional landscapes. (Gordon, 1957, p. 91; and, 1979, p. 273).

7

ANIMAL CONGREGATION AT GARDEN AND REGROWTH SITES

ALTHOUGH regrowth vegetation provides a large number of useful plants, it is of still greater importance to Guaymí livelihood indirectly, because of the increased populations of certain animal species which it supports—the latter being a major Guaymí food resource.

Though tropical rainforest is notoriously productive, this impression of high productivity is accentuated by the large standing crop. Actually, annual biomass production is probably even greater in some stages of secondary growth than in the forest itself. Furthermore, the vegetable biomass of early secondary growth (and of gardens) is in a form more available for animal use than is that of the forest. New regrowth with its numerous herbaceous and large-leaved species contains relatively little cellulose and a larger percentage of readily digestible tissue. Such leafy tissue supports numerous herbivorous insects, and these in turn attract birds, reptiles, etc. A good example is the *patatilla,* a common weed of lowland gardens and recently abandoned fields. The plant is apparently delectable for all sorts of herbivores. Few of its leaves reach their full size without being thoroughly perforated by feeding insects. Near rivers iguanas come inland from the banks to feed on it. And the leaves are eaten by deer and peccaries as well.

Although the actual number of insect species is no doubt smaller in young regrowth and garden than in forests, populations of the regrowth species are greatly increased. As a result, insectivorous birds are common in every abandoned clearing and garden: king birds, kiskadees, wrens, gnatcatchers, etc. Yellow and white butterflies (colors rare in the forest) swarm in sunny clearings; damsel flies and fireflies are abundant too. Lizards and snakes are especially abundant in regrowth. Boas, drawn to regrowth in the vicinity of homesites by increased populations of small mammals and birds, raid chicken pens there. The numerous bats in the Indian huts are further evidence of the large insect populations in clearings; at dawn sleepers waken to the sound of bats fluttering overhead as they search out roosts in the darkness of the roof thatch. Termites build large nests on and near decaying tree stumps and trunks (Indian boys often hack off chunks of their nests and carry them home to throw to the poultry, which feed on the swarming insects). That leafcutter ants (*Atta*) are most common at agricultural and regrowth sites, has been noted in several parts of Panama; furthermore, as plant succession proceeds, the ants become "less abundant until, in very old forests, *Atta* colonies are very hard to find" (Haines,

Leaf-cutter ants, *Atta,* use flowers and leaves to culture fungi in subterranean chambers. An ant can carry up to 30 times its own weight. (R. Buchsbaum)

1975, p. 108). (The very intensive pruning done by leafcutters may be of some importance in the seasonal development of regrowth and other plants. The ants are particularly fond of the flowers of the tropical almond; when the tree is blooming the ants almost ignore its leaves, while whole lines of ants can be seen carrying away its tiny flowers—each ant carrying an entire blossom. Seagrape trees which have been recently stripped by ants appear to bear fruit at a different season from their neighbors.)

Plants which produce small seeds (e.g. various monocots), are especially numerous in young secondary growth; thus various gramivorous birds, absent in the forest, are attracted to clearings. More important, the great concentrations of plants with fleshy fruits such as the madders and the melastomes attract insects, frugivorous birds, squirrels, etc. Furthermore, plants with large starchy roots—rare in the forest—are among the principal garden plants and well represented in new regrowth. Garden plants such as manioc and the three-leaved yam often survive for some time in regrowth, supplying food there for paca, peccary, and agouti populations. Regrowth yam and wild sweet potato are among the plants of new regrowth which add to this starch supply.

And finally, the reduced seasonality of regrowth vegetation means that the fruit of various plants may be available as animal food throughout the year.

One of the best examples of the effect of regrowth vegetation upon animal life is a small tree called the *guarumo*. No tree is more characteristic of regrowth in the American tropics. Although direct human uses of *guarumo* are few, the tree is a notoriously heavy producer of animal food. For example, "Monkeys, sloths, woodpeckers, honeycreepers, and many other birds. Azteca leaf-eating insects, and at times even Atta ants ..." feed on it (Skutch, 1945). The *guarumo* is rare in undisturbed forest but growing as it does in dense stands in regrowth it represents a comparatively concentrated food supply there for such animals as favor it.

Not only do certain animals thrive within the regrowth itself but others, e.g., such edge-species as toucans and the brocket deer, frequent nearby surrounding forest in larger than normal numbers.

In the Guaymí area the fact that clearings may be made and abandoned at any time of the year means that all stages of succession are in existence simultaneously in close proximity to each other (not so in areas where clearing is done only in a dry season)—thus the variety of animal food is maximized. As seen from the coast, forest-covered hills here are mottled various shades of green by regrowth at different stages of development.

Mammals

ARMADILLOS, one of the most commonly taken Guaymí game animals, are more numerous in *rastrojo* than in forest; they are also frequently caught in gardens, which are usually pitted with holes dug in capturing them. The spiny rat, common both in gardens and young regrowth, is rarely caught in heavy forest. Rabbits, among the more common mammals in gardens, are also found in both young and old regrowth. The red squirrel is especially common in tree gardens: It is a pest in cacao orchards and even in coconut groves; the squirrel is the only animal here that can climb coconut trees and gnaw through the nut's husk and shell.

Nine-banded armadillo. (R. Buchsbaum)

The agouti, a voracious herbivore, is found both in forest and regrowth. Within the forest agoutis live in holes in the ground, often at the bases of trees. They congregate near food sources and often raid crop plants in gardens. The agouti is known to be a principal seed-dispersing agent in these forests; almost certainly it is the most important seed-dispersing mammal. Agoutis have the habit of "scatter hoarding," which is to say "they carry individual seeds for distances of up to 50 m and bury them without damage" (Smythe, 1970, p. 32). They are great gnawers, and in the forest often feed on, and carry about, seeds with heavy woody coverings; for example, they will even eat the seeds of the sea bean (*Entada*), a large liana frequently found in old regrowth. Because of its "scatter hoarding," the agouti is critically important in succession, and its presence is probably essential for reestablishment of a number of large-seeded forest trees in clearings during the later stages of regrowth.

An agouti kept as a Guaymí pet. Agoutis make much use of their front feet, holding up food like a squirrel, and cleaning head and ears in a scrubbing motion. The animal has to be kept on a tether because when placed in a wooden cage, it immediately sets about gnawing its way out. Agoutis eat a great variety of vegetable foods; for example, this one accepted orange seeds.

The collared peccary, or *zahino,* is another animal found both in forest and *rastrojo.* It raids plantations frequently, and is usually hunted at garden edges in the early mornings.

The paca (confusingly here called *conejo,* i.e. "rabbit" in Spanish) is a semi-aquatic rodent. Where gardens are made in the vicinity of water it may be a pest, e.g. digging up manioc roots. The paca feeds mainly during the night. Along the coast Bocatoreños hunt it successfully with flashlights or headlamps, and a few Guaymí have begun to do the same.

Red spider monkey, *Ateles geoffroyi.* (R. Buchsbaum)

Birds

THERE ARE PROBABLY few comparable areas with a larger number of bird species than Panama. Colombia is credited with having close to the largest number of nesting birds of any country in the western hemisphere—some 1398 species. Panama has slightly less than half that number. But taking its comparatively small size into account (about one-fifteenth the size of Colombia), Panama is probably unrivalled in terms of the average number of bird species to be found per square kilometer. And in Bocas del Toro Province, where forested hills (dotted with gardens surrounded by all stages of regrowth) approach rich riparian and coastal habitats, the variety of bird life is indeed remarkable.

Studies in various parts of the American tropics have shown that generally regrowth bird species are sharply distinguished from those of surrounding forest—birds of mature forest being poor at invading second growth. Furthermore, just as streamsides are a principal source of *rastrojo* plants in Bocas del Toro Province, it has been established in many tropical areas that "riparian bird species contribute disproportionately to the faunas of second growth" (Terborgh, 1975, p. 370). For example, in settled areas the little tinamou is usually found in the regrowth on old fields, but "where extensive stands of tall forest still remain, it ranges mainly near the banks of streams" (Whitmore, 1972, p. 19).

While the great tinamou roosts in and eats the fruit of tall forest trees, its relative the little tinamou lives in riparian vegetation or second growth; there it sleeps and feeds on the ground, its food consisting of seeds and insects (Skutch, 1963, p. 224). The preferred habitat of each species is identified by its Spanish name: *perdice de montaña* (i.e., of the forest) being the great tinamou, while the little tinamou is called *perdice de rastrojo*. Similarly, the curassow, and to a lesser degree the guan, are birds of the heavy forest while the related, but smaller, gray-headed chachalaca is found here only in regrowth.

The tinamou builds a crude nest on the ground in the forest. It utters a plaintive melodic cry. (R. Buchsbaum)

The toucans tend to be "edge birds," particularly the chestnut-billed toucan. On the other hand, the keel-billed toucan and the collared aricari are not only present in forest edges but in tree gardens and regrowth as well.

Keel-billed toucan. (R. Buchsbaum)

Woodpeckers are especially common in tree gardens because of the number of insects and tree stumps found there; for example, the large and colorful lineated woodpecker. Away from shoreline several flycatchers, e.g. the social flycatcher, the common tody and tropical kingbird are virtually limited to clearings and second growth; on the other hand woodcreepers are almost confined to mature forest.

In June the scaled pigeon can be found nesting scattered about in tree gardens and regrowth. But in February and March the birds congregate and fly together to feed on the fruits of *nance del monte, oreja de mula,* and other *rastrojo* plants. The pigeon flocks also descend to the coast and eat seagrapes and cocoplums. Farther inland, the short-billed pigeon, or *guarumero,* a slightly smaller bird, also flocks seasonally to feed in the regrowth, especially—as the bird's name suggests—upon fruits of the *guarumo* tree.

Birds observed in a Guaymí Tree Garden and in Surrounding Regrowth on the Lower Río San Pedro in mid-January, 1978

English	Guaymí	Bocatoreño	Scientific
banana quit	**usurí**	*uish-uish*	*Coereba flaveola*
bay wren	**chogilí**	*chárra*	*Thryothorus nigricapillus*
black-cowled oriole			*Icterus prosthemelas*
black-crested jay	**sun-sun**		*Cyanocorax affinis*
black-striped sparrow		*chichimero*	*Arremonops conirostris*
blue-gray tanager	**muróvi**	*azulejo*	*Thraupis episcopus*
blue ground dove	**udu-chí**		*Claravis pretiosa*
blue-headed parrot	**sulí**	*casanga*	*Pionus menstruus*
buff-throated saltator	**zíro**		*Saltator maximus*
collared aracari	**bisi-lí**		*Pteroglossus torquatus*
great kiskadee	**súzu**		*Pitangus suphuratus*
keel-billed toucan	**kueré**		*Ramphastos sulfuratus*
lineated woodpecker	**sigle**		*Dryocopus lineatus*
little tinamou	**suéra**		*Crypturellus soui*
montezuma oropendola	**ñuri**	*yellow tail*	*Gymnostinops montezuma*
orange-billed sparrow	**segendú**		*Arremon aurantiirostris*
orange-crowned oriole			*Icterus auricapillus*
ruddy ground dove	**udu**		*Columbina talpacoti*
rufous-tailed hummingbird	**mi-chí**		*Amazilia tzacatl*
scarlet-rumped tanager	**lóba**		*Ramphocelus paserinii*
tropical kingbird	**suzu-kiadri**		*Tyrranus melancholicus*
yellow-billed cacique	**uá-gado**	*pico plata*	*Amblycercus holosericeus*
yellow-rumped tanager	**buru-sógua**	*bananero*	*Ramphocelus icteronotus*
yellow-tailed oriole	**ñoro**	*parao*	*Icterus mesomelas*

The ruddy ground dove, the black-headed saltator, and the black-striped sparrow are among the birds which are almost confined here to young regrowth and gardens. The ruddy ground dove especially favors low stubble where tree gardens have been cleared with the machete; there, the doves can often be seen, e.g. in July, picking up pieces of straw and small sticks to build nests in the branches of fruit trees overhead. Other birds, such as the black-thighed gross-beak, are especially common at the borders of surrounding forest.

Note the predominance of fruit-eating species in the list—tanagers, orioles, caciques and toucans. These are the most abundant birds in spite of the fact that they are those most heavily hunted. Small frugivorous birds are a major Guaymí food source; this is true because on the one hand these species find a rich supply of food in the regrowth, and on the other because they have remarkably high reproductive rates. The only place where I have seen small bird life seriously depleted by Guaymí hunters is in the lower Cricamola Valley—an atypical area with large numbers of Indians in transit for Almirante and Changuinola to work for the Company.

Almost as commonly present as the frugivorous birds are the insect eaters—though some of these, e.g. the kiskadee, actually eat fruit too. Doves and sparrows, often primarily seed eaters elsewhere, also depend heavily upon fruit here—especially the orange-billed sparrow which is actually caught in traps baited with fruit. Similarly, the buff-throated saltator, a finch, is one of the worst banana pests; and the black-crested jay eats peachpalm fruit, bananas, and other fruit.

A real challenge to the bird hunter is the yellow-billed cacique, a black, robin-sized bird with a light bill. It is among the more common garden birds, where it skulks through shrubbery even close to houses; though hard to get in full view, it is seemingly always present. (Of the birds listed, the only one which is not common here is the orange-crowned oriole; as far as I know it has not been reported from this area, being best known from eastern Panama.) The little tinamou's call is unmistakable; though frequently heard in these tracts of regrowth, it is rarely seen.

The blue-gray tanager and the blue-headed parrot are among the worst pests on ripening peachpalm fruits. Because blue-headed parrots are such a pest in tree gardens, the Guaymí follow their movements with special interest, and prepare to drive them off. The birds can be heard at a distance as they approach to raid peachpalm groves. They travel in small flocks, chattering continuously amongst themselves as they fly—a sound to which Guaymí ears are well attuned. The parrots are apparently more startled by the human voice than by actual sight of human figures; and on occasion, though it may well come as a surprise to visitors here, everyone in a normally quiet Guaymí household may suddenly break out shouting at the top of his voice. The parrots undertake their forays with what the Guaymí describe as an exasperating intelligence; and indeed the chatter within parrot flocks, as the birds are driven from garden to garden, does sound rather like a conspiratorial plotting of maneuvers.

The parrot is also a great pest in maize plots, along with the montezuma oropendola, or "yellow tail." Blue ground doves are especially common where the Indians raise rice, sometimes coming to the doorsteps to feed on winnowings. Such garden and regrowth birds are eaten with but few exceptions. The bay wren, which acts as a noisy housewatcher, is not eaten; nor are quail and their eggs; nor whip-poor-wills, for some reason. Nor do they eat several downriver bird species which have arrived here recently in association with Bocatoreño settlers. Because natural history and daily life are so completely interwoven here, interest in local plant and animal life is deep; many Indians are excellent naturalists. I had with me a book which fascinated the Guaymí and stimulated hours of discussion: R.S. Ridgely's *A Guide to the Birds of Panama,* finely illustrated by J.A. Gwynne. It was curious to see how, not content with simply viewing the birds on its pages, older people ran their fingers over the illustrations—often with appreciative chuckles—as if to sense the detail more completely.

Bird Dissemination of Regrowth Plants

LARGE-SEEDED PLANTS are more characteristic of forests than of regrowth. "Many trees characteristic of the older forest bear seeds that are much more massive than those typical of secondary growth" (Smythe, 1970, p. 32). Many of these large seeds are spread throughout the forest by mammals.

Regrowth vegetation, on the other hand, includes a great assortment of plants bearing small, fleshy fruits. For most of these plants, birds are the principal agents of dissemination. Thus, forest-clearing initiates a reciprocal, mutually expansive, relationship; the number of fruit-eating birds and the total area of berry-producing regrowth shrubs increasing together. Take the panama-hat plant and its fruits for example: "Although these mucilaginous fruits are almost tasteless to the human tongue, they are eagerly devoured by birds," among which, in Costa Rica, a "black tanager with a scarlet rump" is one of the plant's disseminators (Skutch, 1949, p. 174). Panama-hat plants and scarlet-rumped tanagers are also among the more common species of Bocas del Toro regrowth.

Huesito (*Faramea* sp.) is a tall shrub or small tree of the madder family, common in old regrowth. Squirrels and birds eat its grape-like fruits; both the skins and flesh of the fruits are deep blue.

Following is a list of regrowth plants with fleshy or berry-like fruits which grow in the lower San Pedro Valley:

Regrowth Shrubs and Small Trees Bearing Fleshy or Berry-like Fruit Eaten by Birds

Bellucia axinthera	Melastomaceae
Byrsonima ssp.	Malpighiaceae
Callicarpa acuminata	Verbenaceae
Campelia zynonia	Commelinaceae
Compsoneura sprucei	Myrsticaceae
Carica sp.	Caricaceae
Carludovica palmata	Cyclanthaceae
Cassipourea elliptica	Rhyzophoraceae
Cecropia ssp.	Moraceae
Centropogon sp.	Campanulaceae
Cephaelis elata	Rubiaceae
Cestrum sp.	Solanaceae
Clidemia septuplinervia	Melastomaceae
Conostegia xalapensis	Melastomaceae
Cordia dwyeri and *C. spinescens*	Boraginaceae
Citharexylum caudatum	Verbenaceae
Faramea sp.	Rubiaceae
Guatteria aeruginosa and *G. lucens* ?	Annonaceae
Heisteria longipes	Olacaceae
Herrania purpurea	Sterculiaceae
Isertia haenkeana	Rubiaceae
Isertia hypoleuca	Rubiaceae
Lantana sp.	Verbenaceae
Marlierea sp.	Myrtaceae
Miconia dolichorryncha	Melastomaceae
Miconia lonchophylla	Melastomaceae
Miconia nutans ?	Melastomaceae
Miconia prasina	Melastomaceae
Miconia simplex	Melastomaceae
Miconia trinervia	Melastomaceae
Neea amplifolia	Nyctaginaceae
Pentagonia macrophylla	Rubiaceae
Phytolacca rivinoides	Phytolaccaceae
Posoqueria latifolia	Rubiaceae
Psychotria polyphlebia	Rubiaceae
Psychotria racemosa	Rubiaceae
Psychotria suerrensis	Rubiaceae
Siparuna pauciflora	Monimiaceae
Tovomita sp.	Guttiferae
Tococa guianensis	Melastomaceae
Vismia macrophylla	Guttiferae
Xylosma sp.	Flacourtiaceae

Madder family regrowth shrub, *Cephaelis*. The family is strongly represented in regrowth vegetation.

Nancillo (Citharexylum caudatum) in the verbena family, collected in Guaymí regrowth along the Río San Pedro. It is also found along the inland edges of beaches. The fruits are an important bird food.

Thus, the list includes more than forty regrowth shrubs and small trees the fruits of which are eaten by birds. A notably large proportion of the plants are of the melastome and madder families. All can be collected from a few patches of regrowth growing within a short distance of each other in the Río San Pedro Valley. Although thorough search of surrounding forest would probably yield an even larger number of fleshy-fruited shrubs and small trees, no such concentrations occur there.

The fruits of yet other regrowth plants here are eaten by birds, e.g. vines (passionflower species) and herbs (such as *Campelia zanonia*).

Although birds are probably the major agent of seed dispersal in regrowth shrubs and small trees, the seeds of several species are spread by wind. Wind dissemination is not common in undisturbed tropical rainforests (monkey pot is one of the exceptions here) but those plants spread in this way may have some advantage in clearings. The *cigarillo* tree is an example. Its large, rectangular, flattened woody pods open in July and release numerous small papery-margined seeds. Wind is also important in the dissemination of composites (a family which appears to be much better represented in clearings than in the forest itself); for instance, a shrubby composite which the Toreños call "jack-in-the-bush" is a very aggressive (and quite useless) weed in coastal gardens. Wind also carries the seeds of the balsa tree and the bignonia-family liana, *Paragonia pyramidata*, from riverbanks to forest clearings.

8

INDIAN SUBSISTENCE AND MATERIAL CULTURE

Regrowth Animals as Food

IT IS THE concentration of small game in tracts of regrowth vegetation, and especially the abundance of birds there, that makes these sites so important to Guaymí subsistence.

In pre-European times, as today, the principal Guaymí meat supply came from hunted rather than domesticated animals. When asked to name their most important game species adult Indians usually and and with a touch of pride, list such large animals as peccary, paca, tapir, brocket deer and curassow. But, considering game resources as a whole, smaller animals are much more important.

The following typical regrowth and garden mammals were listed for me as having been killed within a period of about two months near a Guaymí household of eight, three adults and five children: two armadillos, two rabbits, a spined rat and a squirrel (the latter is one of the worst pests on *pataste* and cacao). Large garden-raiding forest animals such as peccaries and pacas are killed only occasionally; none were killed within this period. On the other hand, small *rastrojo* birds were killed on an almost daily basis.

Notes on Diet and Food Preservation

A TYPICAL MEAL in a Guaymí household is a calabash heaped with starchy food: boiled bananas, manioc, dasheen, yam, yautia, etc. Mashed ripe bananas mixed in a calabash bowl with cold water is a common after-meal drink. It is not quantity that is lacking but balance. Large amounts of boiled greens are often served, too, and these add nutrients; for example, they probably supply calcium.

But protein, particularly, is in short supply. Protein-rich foods may not be available in regularly served meals for days on end. Servings of peach palm fruit, which contains some protein, are mainly confined to that tree's harvest season. Occasionally one of the larger game animals is killed, and then there is something of a feast. The Guaymí keep few domesticated animals; thus, there are an irregular source of meat. Pigs, ducks and chickens are the most important. Chickens, prone to disease and easy victims of wild predators, are seldom kept in large numbers. The Indians are reluctant to kill a pig for their own use, that animal being their most dependable product for sale so that they may obtain machetes, cloth, kerosene and salt. (In trade, pigs have the great advantage that they can be walked out of the forest, rather than having to be carried as do most products, e.g. rice.)

Because it is not stored in the human body a sustained source of protein is required in small amounts on an almost daily basis for a balanced diet. It is especially necessary for the health of growing children, but is often lacking at Guaymí family meals. Under these circumstances Guaymí children are dedicated meat-morsel hunters, engaged in a daily quest for protein-rich foods, particularly in regrowth vegetation and gardens. Their needs are met by the frequent eating of small birds or fishes, lizards, snails, frogs, etc. Among the more common of the several edible lizards in gardens and regrowth is the **dre-kunga,** *Basilicus vittatus.*

Preparation of the catch is simple and efficient: it requires no utensils or water, and can be done by a six-year-old child. Some animals can be prepared without even a knife, the guts being stripped with a finger. The animal is then wrapped in two layers of fresh wild banana leaves, and children usually carry this small package to the house and lay it in the hearth against coals still glowing from the last family meal, for roasting. Adult Guaymí often do the same thing; capture of small birds is not beneath their dignity. Even the banana quit and hummingbird, each scarcely a mouthful, are hunted.

At one Guaymí household on the Río San Pedrito, two children snared, plucked, cleaned, wrapped and roasted three orange-billed sparrows and then went out and caught a third, all in the course of my afternoon's conversation with their parents. Such small frugivorous birds appear to have remarkably high reproductive rates, since they remain abundant despite such persistent hunting. Children systematically rob bird nests, too. Boiled eggs are a common gift to visitors; for instance a Guaymí boy came to me with half a dozen boiled eggs of the white-throated crake. A number of bird species tolerate removal of their eggs, replenishing the nest several times before finally rebuilding it elsewhere.

The Guaymí place less emphasis on food preservation than do peoples in areas which have greater variations in abundance. To be sure, food storage is difficult in this environment. For instance, pests are numerous. The omnipresent cockroach makes keeping food even overnight a major problem; every tidbit must be placed in a container of some sort—commonly in packages made of folded green leaves of wild bananas. Though food spoils quickly, an attempt is made to keep surpluses after seasons of plenty. Preservation methods include smoking, drying in the sun or over fire, parching, and fermenting.

The *barbacoa,* the prototype of our barbeque, is an old aboriginal device for smoking meat in tropical America. Meat is placed on a frame above a slow fire—the flesh being simultaneously smoked, dried, and partially cooked. If the animal is small the Guaymí simply clean and skin it, and then suspend it in the smoke with a string.

Minnows may be sun-dried, for example, *titi* fry. But since rainy weather is common, fry are often spread on green wild banana leaves, layer upon layer, and

Toucans are among the more common Indian game birds, particularly the keel-billed toucan, the larger bird in the photograph. (Its beak is multi-colored, mainly yellow, red and blue with a black belt at its base.) Keel-billed toucans are especially common in regrowth vegetation and tree gardens, and are probably responsible for the re-seeding of a number of forest plants in clearings, various species of palm for example. In July the birds feed heavily upon the walnut-sized fruits of the *sangre* (which contains large, scarlet-coated seeds) and the *cocoita,* trees common at forest edges and in old regrowth. The toucans are also often seen feeding upon the fruits of the polewood and the *carachero* which are also regrowth trees.

The smaller bird in the photograph is a collared aracari. (Its upper bill is gray with a black tip, the bird's head being black with red spots behind the eyes.) Like the keel-billed toucan, the collared aracari is found mainly in second growth woods. Related birds, the chestnut-mandibled toucan and the yellow-eared toucanet are also hunted here but these, particularly the toucanet, are forest species.

dried over a slow fire instead. They are then ground and stored (usually these days in bottles). Such fish meal keeps poorly, but for some time after the *titi* season has ended it may be added to the usual Guaymí fare of starchy roots.

Quantities of parched cornmeal are carried in gourds on long trips; mixed with fresh stream water at rest-stops, it makes a refreshing and nourishing drink.

As noted earlier, various fermented beverages are made from maize, peach-palm fruit, manioc, hog plums and sapodilly fruit. A particularly interesting use of the fermentation process in food preservation involves the storage of peach-palm fruit. The Guaymí store this fruit in pit-silos. Such pits are made throughout Guaymí country. A hole is dug about 1 m^2 in cross-section and 1 m deep. The bottom and sides are carefully lined with wild banana leaves. The ripe fruit is put into the hole, uncooked, and then covered with more leaves and dirt. The fruit, partly fermented, is dug up, cooked and eaten when food is scarce. It may be dug up as much as a year later. The taste changes slightly, having a sour-sweet flavor. (Such stored palm fruit is often used, too, in making a beverage.) Pits dug under houses keep the fruit especially well but pits are also made in well-drained ground elsewhere. The procedure is interestingly similar to that used in preserving poi and sweet potatoes on the Pacific Islands (Sonderstrom, p. 238), and also brings to mind the subterranean food storage chambers (*chultunes*) used by the ancient Maya. Preserving peach palm by drying and smoking, noted among the Guaymí in the early 17th century (Salcedo, p. 86), is also practiced today, but the method is less effective than is fermentation in pit-silos.

Hunting and Fishing Equipment

FALL-TRAPS, weighted with heavy rocks, are placed on forest and *rastrojo* trails especially for killing armadillos, these being slow-moving animals. (They are called "ground hogs" by English-speakers in the Province). Agoutis are caught in boxlike enclosures; a rock-weighted, wooden, lid-like frame falls into place when the agouti gets inside and trips a release. Agoutis, pacas, armadillos, and peccaries are all taken in another trap consisting of a large net like a carrying bag, but made to open widely, which is spread on the ground. The bag has a cinch-cord by which it can be drawn quickly together. A sapling is bent over, fastened to the cord, and locked with a release trigger. When an animal walks across the net and trips the release, it is enveloped and hoisted into the air. But by far the most common animal trap, used especially for catching birds, is the loop snare. Various small mammals are also caught with these snares.

Birds are sometimes taken in yet another kind of trap: small sticks are painted with the latex of the *negrito* tree after the sap has been heated in the sun to concentrate it. These sticks are then tied to some tree which produces a fruit much eaten by birds. The sticks are scattered around in the branches where the feeding birds will brush against them. Thrashing about, they may become stuck to several sticks. Even large birds are caught in this way.

Guaymí boys, and men as well, often carry slingshots and pockets full of pebbles, and are constantly trying for small birds.

In addition to using fish poison and wicker traps, the Guaymí take fish with bow and arrow. Or they are speared: a cane-like palm (*Geonoma calyptrogynoidea*) is a choice material for fish spears. The palm stems are straight, 3-5 meters long, roughly 3 cm in diameter, and very hard. (The stems are also used by the Bókata in making carrying frames.)

Guaymí loop snare for catching small birds, made by bending a sapling over, fastening it to a looped cord and locking it with a release trigger. Such snares, baited with fruit, can be seen in every tree garden and scattered along trails through regrowth.

Fish-spearing is a skill upon which the Guaymí pride themselves—though, in fact, much larger quantities of fish are taken with nets and fish-poison. The basic historical and economic significance of fish and fish-spearing can be seen in the traditional Guaymí stick game, where contestants pretend to be spearing fish and call out this fish or that one—as they cast balsa shafts at each other's legs.

Further indication of the fundamental importance of the fish in Guaymí culture is the frequent reference to the animal in other lore and ritual. When a Guaymí dies, relatives and friends gather, men sitting at one side of the meeting place, women at the other. A calabash of water scented with *culantro* and with

The common three-pronged Guaymí fish spear, made of fire-hardened peach palm wood, on the right. It is also used for killing birds, though it often sticks in the tree branches. A kind of heavy, blunt-tipped arrow, the metal taken from a worn-out machete blade is used for larger game. Bows are also made from peach palm wood. The San Blas make a very similar three-pronged spear.

Guaymí dip nets, used in taking small fish and, particularly, shrimp such as the **kebé,** common in sluggish coastal streams. The netting is the same as that used in carrying-bags. Often the nets are colorfully dyed.

several little fish (**bidigá**) swimming in it, is passed along the line of mourners. Each person puts a finger into the water, then touches it to his tongue. The fish are then freed in the nearest stream, supposedly taking the spirit and all bad memories of the dead person with them.

Dip-nets are made of the same wild pineapple webbing as is used in making carrying bags. Or, since many nets are sometimes needed in a hurry for catching schools of fish such as the *titi,* makeshift nets are made also from the fruit sheathes of *guagara* palms—so that everyone can participate quickly in the catch. Wicker traps with a funnel-shaped entrance are made too; these being placed in shallow water near stream banks and a ditch dug leading to their entrance.

Large marine fish are now caught on metal hooks purchased in stores. But fish hooks were used here aboriginally as well. Columbus's son Ferdinand noted fish hooks which the Indians here "make out of turtle shells, cutting them by means of *cabuya* [i.e. wild pineapple] fibers, in the manner of one sawing" (Sauer, 1966, p. 132).

Two of the ways in which Guaymí around Cusapín sometimes catch fish nowadays may seem rather impractical. In one, several women walk out into a quiet surf with a sheet and holding its edges, dip it into a school of small fish. Then they lift the sheet, sloshing the water out in such a way that the fish are left behind. In the other way, two boys ride in a dugout canoe; the boy in back paddles slowly and quietly; the one in front sits facing him with a machete in his hand. When the boat is guided into a school of small fish, the boy with the machete swings it around slowly in a broad circle, allowing the blade to dip deeply into the water. At each dip several small fish, partly cut through, are brought up strung along the machete's edge and are shaken off into the bottom of the boat to be used as bait.

Other Artifacts and Customs

THE GUAYMI make carrying bags out of an exceptionally strong, fine fiber obtained from the wild pineapple plant. They are the only people in Bocas del Toro Province who cultivate the plant and make such bags.

Only women are involved in the manufacture. The leaves of the plant are scraped with a blade-like, sharp-edged stick to remove all soft tissue, leaving behind only the fibers, which are bleached in the sun. A bundle of the whitened fiber, held at one end by the toes, is combed with the fingers, separating and straightening the individual strands. Instead of using a spindle in making such thread, the women roll the fibers between the palm of a hand and a thigh. A white powder, made of the dried latex of the *chutra* tree, is first sprinkled over thigh and hand to make the thread twist tightly. A two-ply twine is made from the thread; it is now often dyed with aniline, but vegetable dyes are much used, too.

The bags are called **kra** in Guaymí; Toreños call them *chacaras.* They are made up of what I think is generally called "coiled netting," that is, a continuous spiral, expanded upward. The coils are simply looped, inverted "e's," not knotted as is most network. The bag starts from an elongated oval of mesh at the bottom, sometimes surrounded by a number of wedge-shaped sections. The coil netting extends upward from this base. The netting is made with the fingers alone, using no needle or other instrument.

The carrying band is a loose braid tied to the bag with loops of twine. It is placed across the head, with the loaded bag itself resting on the carrier's lower back.

This carrying bag is the most distinctive of Guaymí artifacts and of basic importance in their livelihood. In fact, from birth every Guaymí starts life in one. They are used as cradles and it is a rare Guaymí household in which at least one cannot be seen hanging from the rafters; when an infant cries someone immediately starts the bag swinging. Mothers carry their babies in the bags wherever they go.

The bags are made in a variety of sizes and have a great deal of stretch, particularly in circumference; vegetable harvests, domesticated animals, and household belongings are also transported or stored in them. Some are very small and finely worked, for instance those used for purses. I have seen no better bags amongst tribes elsewhere in Central America.

Guaymí household. Note the carrying bag used as a cradle.

Guaymí women near the Rio Cricamola. Women often have broad depressions across their skulls made by the headbands of carrying bags.

Guaymí woman travelling the beach near the Río Chiriquí in the rain with her carrying bag covered with the leaves of the panama-hat plant.

Along the Atlantic coast Guaymí and Térraba houses rest on piles a few feet above the ground. They have a rectangular hiproof of thatch and the floors are made from slats of split palm trunks. A notched log serves as a stairway. Inside the house, fastened to the wall several feet above the floor, is a bench or platform which is divided by cane partitions to form little cagelike sleeping quarters.

On the upper Atlantic slopes and on the Pacific side, most Guaymí houses have dirt floors and conical roofs. Several heavy crotched poles are set into the ground and a frame of cross pieces is built on their crotched ends approximately seven feet above the ground. A conical lean-to of thin poles is built above this frame and tied on, then thatched. In very large houses a long heavy pole set in the middle of the floor extends to the top of the structure, with supports extending at intervals between this central pole and the roof. The apex of the roof is made of sedge drawn together, bent over, and tied. Sedge is cultivated for this and other uses. Some houses have pots placed over the sedge of the apex. Housetops in the savannas often have Christian crosses affixed.

Both of these house types are probably aboriginal in Panama. Most definitely so is the type with conical roof and dirt floor found in places distant from European influences, as on the upper Río Cricamola and Río Caña.

Along the Caribbean coast the elevated, rectangular-roofed house is common among mestizo people, and is replacing the conical-roofed type sometimes found among the Guaymí and Bókata thereabouts. On the Pacific slope, too, for instance between Tolé and Cañazas, the Guaymí who live close to mestizo settlements make houses with rectangular roofs, but with dirt floors.

Climatic environment alone does not determine the choice of house type; instead the type often expresses tribal tradition. True, dirt floors would be less practical in areas of continual rain, as on the Atlantic slope, but other factors, such as the types of domesticated animals raised, are more important. For example, pile dwellings have become more widespread since the introduction of the European pig. On the Atlantic slope, pigs, which are the principal domesticated animal, are sheltered beneath the floor. On the Pacific slope, where the Guaymí raise cattle, a wall is formed by pounding stakes around the dirt floor just under the edge of the conical roof to keep the cattle out; a break is left in the circle for an entrance.

Standing outside many of the houses is a sort of skull rack, a branched stick upon which skulls of mammals and birds killed as game are mounted and saved; this is the survival, perhaps, of earlier custom in which human skulls were saved. The keeping of trophy skulls was noted along this coast by the first Spanish (Sauer, 1966, p. 132) and human skulls were at one time displayed this way among the Mayas (where the trait was perhaps a Toltec influence), and elsewhere.

Guaymí houses usually have two hearths, one for those considered to be in normal health and one for others, e.g., all sick people and pregnant or menstruating women. Food for the latter is cooked on the special hearth and they eat a diet consisting of small fish and certain birds, without salt.

Guaymí house on the Pacific slope near the crest of the Serranía de Tabasará, near Agua Salud. This house type is almost identical to one shown at Natá in Oviedo's original manuscript (reproduced in Lothrop's *Cocle, An Archaeological Study* ..., figure 5, page 15).

Inside the conical thatch roof of a Sabanero-Guaymí house near Agua Salud.

Térraba house on the Río Teribe. The Térraba say that they formerly made their houses round, like those made in the remote territory of the Guaymí; but none are made round today. Thus, the pictured house type appears to be gaining favor among coastal Indians.

Térraba roof thatch. Palm leaflets tied to poles and uniformly spaced makes an especially good thatch. Various South American tribes, e.g. the Yanomamo also make their roof thatch in this way.

A Guaymí flute, made of 25-cm segment of wild cane. Four oval stops have been burned in the upper surface and a thumb hole in the lower. The distal end is open; the proximal end is partially plugged with a black wax and a rectangular hole is cut in the upper surface. Similar flutes, of jaguar bone, are used at the stick games. Such flutes link people of this area with southern cultures; they are found only in S. America and Panama. They have also been described among Teribes and Cuna. The flute-type probably originated in northern S. America. The Guaymí may have learned hat-making from now-extinct neighboring tribes since the craft is better developed among the Cholos in western Veraguas and among mestizo people on Azuero Peninsula. The technique may be derived from Colombia where descendants of the Zenú tribe make the finest specimens of this type of hat.

Palm slat flooring and coarse net hammock made of tree bast. Neither the Térraba nor the Guaymí make much use of the hammock, though it is in fact a native American invention—widely used elsewhere in the Caribbean area. They sleep instead on a sleeping mat made of pounded tree bark thrown on the slat floor. Sleeping mats were needed by the Térraba in even larger numbers when they lived in the old style round houses with dirt floors, as do inland Guaymí today.

A newly-made Térraba drum similar to those made by the Talamanca Indians. The iguana skin to be used as the drum head is folded on top. The Térraba make another type of drum which they refer to as more traditionally their own; it is undistinguishable from the Guaymí drum.

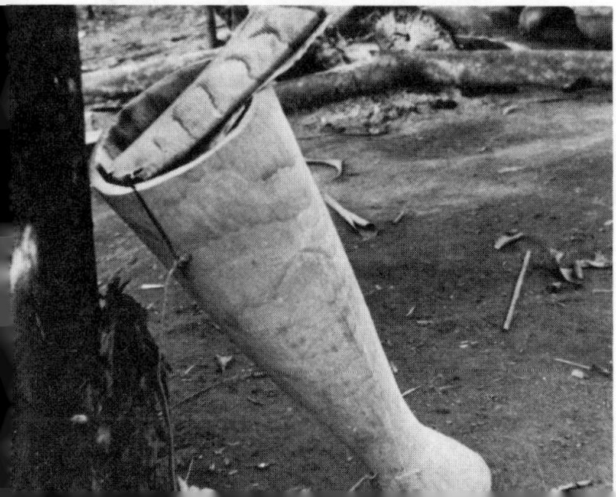

Guaymí skin drum made of a section of balsa log and tied with lianas and wild pineapple fiber.

With building materials close at hand and building skills possessed by practically everyone, houses are frequently replaced. For example, the family of a deceased person leaves the house, to return after nine days for a feast. They then leave again for months, perhaps permanently. Guaymí and Bókata families often have several dwellings and move from one to another, as convenience in caring for crops dictates.

Some Guaymí still practice polygamy, despite prolonged efforts of missionaries to rid them of the custom. Another ancient culture trait, known over a good part of the world at one time, is still held to obsessively by Guaymí, and to a lesser extent, Térraba, in inland areas: a man and his mother-in-law will go to great lengths to avoid seeing each other. In families that I travelled with, this was managed while visiting by draping bark cloth, or sheets, between compartments of the houses. An elderly Térraba told me that disregard for this custom had been for him one of the more distasteful changes of recent years.

I think that the tooth-filing among native people here is another trait linking them with the Mayan area—not an introduced African trait as has been suggested (Stewart, 1942, p. 328). Negroes in this area do not file their teeth, and I find no record of their ever having done so. Although it has not been shown to be a pre-Columbian practice in Panama, the custom was known elsewhere in aboriginal America. For example, among the ancient Tarascans a notch was made in the middle of each incisor: "On a few of the Tarasco skulls the teeth were filed, incisions that made them look like swallowtails having been made in the front teeth." (Lumholtz, 1902, II, p. 427). Many of the Guaymí, the Bókata, and the Cholos along the Veraguas border also file their teeth, but to only one point. Westward in Costa Rica, the Brunka did likewise, until recently. The fashion of filing among the Mayans seems to have been the same as in Bocas del Toro Province, since from early descriptions it appears to have been the corners of the teeth that were removed: "They [the Mayan women] had a custom of filing their teeth, leaving them like the teeth of a saw, and this they considered elegant. Old women performed this task, filing them with certain stones and water" (Landa, vol. 18, p.125).

Cholo youth with filed teeth. Tooth-filing here is more a process of chipping than of actual filing. Usually a piece of metal, say the flat of a dull knife, is placed against the back of a tooth while the front is tapped with a stone.

The stick game, or *balsería* as it is called by other Panamanians, is one of the features of Guaymí culture which has attracted the most attention from outsiders. Contestants cast balsa wood shafts at each other's legs, the game proceeding according to formal and complicated, but decidedly controversial, rules. Many descriptions of these games have been written (the best of which is probably Johnson's, as recorded in Lothrop, 1950, pp. 101-102). The game is permeated with symbols of the Guaymís' close ties with nature: contestants wear the stuffed skins of wild animals (e.g., ocelots) tied to their backs. Spectators wear necklaces of jaguar teeth and hats decorated with anteater hair. They blow conch-shell trumpets and whistles of jaguar bone, rub turtle-shell sound boxes, etc.

Spectators of a stick game, *balseria*, between the Sabanero-Guaymí and the Valientes, being held at Hogli. The plume-like tail hairs of the giant anteater are used as decorations for the men's hats. Jaguar-tooth necklaces are much valued. Cow's horns for trumpets are traded from the savannas of Chiriquí Province.

Horns of conch shell were described here long ago by Peter Martyr (Sauer, 1966, p. 132). They are still the Guaymí's main ceremonial instrument, though these days cow-horn trumpets, obtained in trade with the savanna Guaymí, are popular. The turtle-shell instruments, made especially for stick games, are actually the entire carapace of a small river turtle; rubbing the palm of the hand against the edge of the empty carapace causes it to resonate and give off a howling sound.

The stick game is an old influence for tribal unity among the Guaymí, bringing them together from throughout their territory. By contrast, those who participate in planting and harvesting *juntas* gather from their home neighborhoods only.

9

MARINE AND LITTORAL RESOURCES

As DESCRIBED ABOVE, marine resources were of great importance to Indians of the area in earlier times when the coast was more accessible to them. Indian subsistence was more complex then, combining more completely resources of the shore with those of the forest.

The Guaymí retreated from the southwest coast of Chiriquí Lagoon and its hinterland forests during the 17th to 18th century period of tribal displacements. In the 19th century Guaymí use of the coast was increasingly limited by Bocatoreño colonization, which spread along the shoreline from its center in the town of Bocas del Toro. (Westward, the Térraba Indians experienced an even more complete exclusion from the coast.) As a result of these changes the Indians lost familiarity with the shore environment. Guaymí knowledge of shore resources is best preserved on Valiente Peninsula, around Bluefields and Cusapín.

In association with a growing Indian political movement, coastal lands are now being resettled, and knowledge of marine resources in the embayment is being renewed. Guaymí settlers from the Cricamola Valley are collecting shellfish in a nearshore environment which can be described as follows: On the seaward side of several islands in the embayment, shoreline is located on old fringing reef, with narrow strips of coral-sand beach present in places. Offshore, small coralline boulders and rocks are scattered over a shelf of dead coral. The shelf's hard surface is interrupted by broad flats of coral sand and silt; these flats are mostly overgrown with turtle and manatee grass. At the outer edge of the fringing reef, often hundreds of meters from shoreline and marked by surf or peaking waves, live coral grows in great variety.

A vertical cross-section from land to sea, taking Careening Cay facing Bastimentos as an example, shows roughly the following zonation of benthic organisms:

Splash zone: The marine shell found at highest elevations is the southern periwinkle. The snail is abundant on the trunks of fallen coconut trees, often as much as a meter above the high tide. (On leeward sides of the islands this periwinkle is found on the roots and leaves of mangroves). Equally common, but at lower levels in the splash zone—as well as in the swash—is the zebra nerite.

Intertidal zone: Where beach is present, buried in the sand near mean-tide level are the small coquina clams, *Donax,* which Toreños call *almejas.* These often form dense colonies, and are gathered by handfuls for chowder.

Growing among coralline rocks in the intertidal zone are magpie shells, measled cowries, and tuberculate chitons. An edible alga, *Bryothamnion seaforthii,* lodges its holdfasts in the rocks' pitted surfaces.

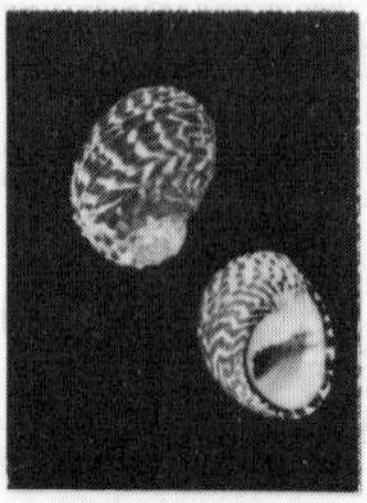

Splash zone:
nerites

Beach sand:
coquinas

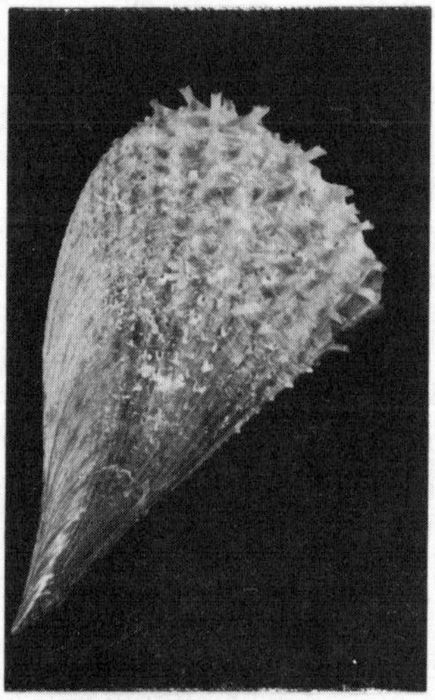

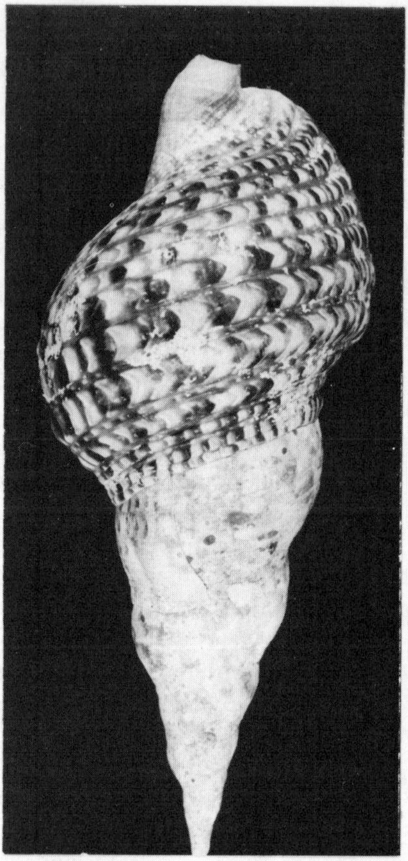

Shallow subtidal: penshell *(left);* trumpet shell *(right).*

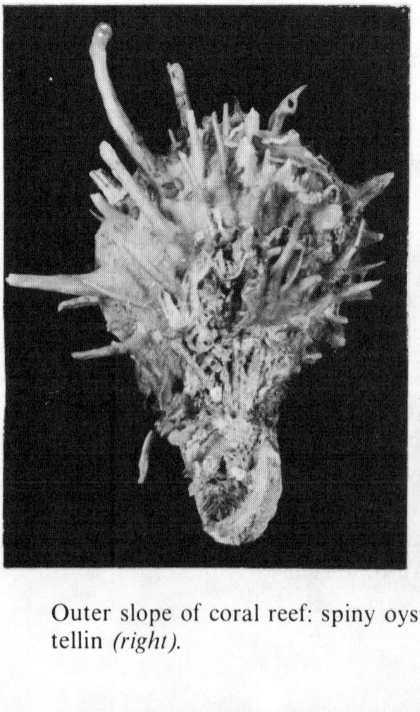

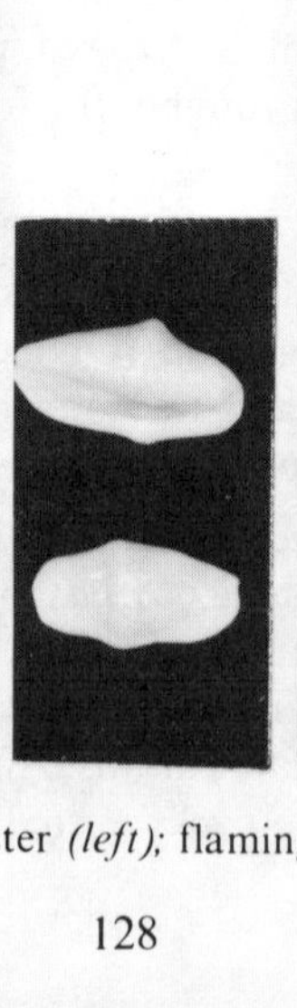

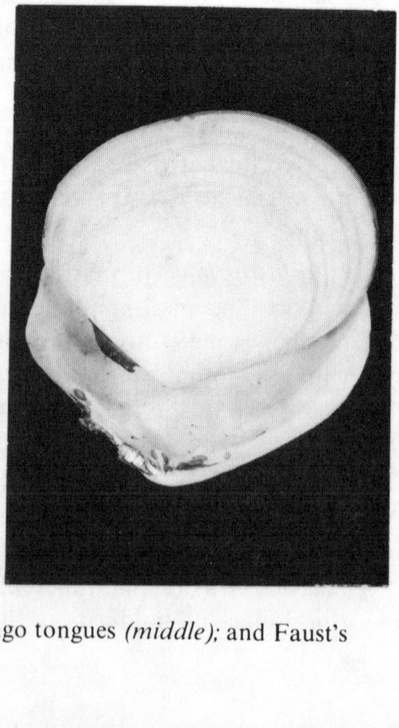

Outer slope of coral reef: spiny oyster *(left);* flamingo tongues *(middle);* and Faust's tellin *(right).*

Shallow subtidal zone: In water which is ankle deep to waist deep at low tide, one finds tulip shells, fighting strombs, trumpet shells and spiny pen shells on sandy bottom, especially in the fields of marine grass; they are easiest seen and collected when they move to patches of bare sand. In slightly deeper water is the well known, and sometimes very large queen stromb, or "broadleaf" as it is called here. As these shells are conspicuous and often picked up by passersby in canoes, one must go a distance from settlements to find large ones. King helmets are found in this zone too, but they are mainly found on the island-sides which face the open sea.

Some shallow subtidal zone species range beyond the outer edge of the fringing reef into deeper water; on the outer slopes of the reefs, they are joined by flamingo tongue, spiny oyster and jewel box.

In the intertidal and shallow subtidal zones, two species of sea urchin are abundant: one, a dark urchin, *Toxopneustes* sp., has white spines; its gonads are eaten raw. The other, *Echinometra oblonga,* reddish-purple, is avoided because its long spines can make a painful wound.

Magpie shells (locally misnamed "whelks"), tulip shells, and fighting strombs are probably the most commonly collected food mollusks on Careening Cay and Bastimentos Island: the magpie, growing near shoreline, is readily available; the tulip is a favorite because of its large proportion of flesh to shell—as is the fighting stromb because of its abundance and size; these are followed in importance by the trumpet shell and queen conch. For the embayment as a whole the fighting stromb and tulip shell are perhaps the most important food species, because of their wide distribution.

Despite the Guaymís' present limited access to parts of the coast, they still catch sea turtles and marine fish (though not in such large quantities as do the Bocatoreños), and take their dugouts miles from shoreline, even beyond Escudo de Veragua. This coast is such a choice turtle hunting area that at one time Indians came all the way from the Mosquito Coast of Nicaragua to catch the animals here.

Four species of sea turtle are found along this coast: the green turtle, the hawksbill, the trunk turtle, and the loggerhead. Of these, the green turtle is by far the most important food species. It rarely lays its eggs here, or even comes to the beach, but passes westward, close inshore, toward Costa Rica where it spawns. Nets are set along offshore coral reefs in 3 m to 6 m of water, to entangle the turtles as they go by. The upper edges of the nets are supported by wooden floats, and the lower weighted with rocks. As the turtle moves westward along the coast, one of its foods is various subtidal algae growing on offshore coral reefs, e.g. *Sargassum filipendula* and *S. fluitans.*

Although some green turtles can be found here between May and September, the big run is in June and, especially, July. In August and September, some of the turtles return from Costa Rica moving eastward, at which time they may enter Chiriquí Lagoon, e.g. in the area around the mouth of the Cricamola River where they feed and fatten in shallow water on the ribbon-like turtle grass.

(People here refer also to a variety of the green turtle called the "yellow," or *blanca*, which is larger than the average and with even tastier flesh; but this may be only a size-class.) A large green turtle will yield seventy or eighty pounds of meat, in 1979 selling in Bocas for forty cents a pound. When the turtles are caught they are brought to the beach, placed on their backs in the shade, and their limbs tied together. In this position they hold their breath for long intervals, as if they were still submerged in the sea; when they exhale it can be heard at a distance and sounds sadly like a giant gasp or sigh. The turtles can be kept like this for days until they are butchered, or picked up by coastal boats which carry them to markets.

The condition of the green turtle population is uncertain; the significance of the unusually small catch in the summer of 1979 was discussed with concern here, by Toreños and Guaymí alike.

The hawksbill arrives here travelling eastward at about the same time that the green turtle passes in the opposite direction so the two are hunted at the same season. Some of the males are taken from the sea in nets, but the ones caught are mostly females coming onto sandy beaches to lay and bury their eggs—at Memeteme beach on the west end of Isla Colón, for example, and in Chiriquí Lagoon, on Escudo de Veragua, and all along this coast from Tabobe eastward to Calovébora and beyond. The eggs are layed in several clutches of decreasing size, at roughly fifteen-day intervals. Sometimes the nests are easily found by following the conspicuous tracks left on the beach by the turtle after she emerges from the water. Twenty years ago in August and September, multitudes of hawksbill hatched here. Most of the young turtles wait until dark to crawl down to the water's edge (fortunately for them, because pelicans and other predators congregate here at this season). Walking the beach near the mouth of the Cricamola River at night with a flashlight one could see the newly-hatched turtles struggling across the sand to the water.

The flesh of hawksbill is strongly flavored and less well-liked than that of the green turtle. The hawksbill has been sought chiefly for its "shell," or carapace. (The shell of the other species has no value.) In the early part of this century tortoise shell, as it was called, was much used in making combs, etc. But plastic materials replaced it for such purposes, and by the 1950s, the shell was worthless—and nearly everyone thought it would remain so. (At that time a lucky elderly Bocatoreña on Chiriquí Lagoon, remembering the old days—and despite her neighbors' amusement—saved a partly-filled room of turtle shell, anticipating a renewal of demand.) The shell is now selling for 15 and 16 dollars a pound. Since a large hawksbill carries three to five pounds of marketable shell, its carapace may be worth between $45 and $75. Unusually large specimens may yield seven pounds of shell. A few years ago one buyer paid $32 per pound for shell for the Japanese market. (Since in drying the shell shrinks by about one-fifth of its weight people along the coast soak it well in water just before taking it to buyers.) Hawksbill flesh sells locally for thirty cents a pound. A female may yield thirty or forty pounds; the male is smaller.

A pair of green turtles, "Bocas Beef" as local English-speakers call it, at the market in Bocas del Toro. The female turtle is in the foreground.

Green turtle and hawksbill aboard a coastal boat bound for Colón in 1968. Such shipment is now illegal.

Some attempt is made to protect the turtles, but it is very difficult to patrol this coast. Both Guaymí and Bocatoreños dig up and eat the eggs, but worse—so do the dogs kept by people who live near the beach. Female hawksbills are caught here in the middle of their laying season: I saw several butchered near Río Chiriquí in 1979, which were still full of eggs. (The animals are placed on their backs and decapitated with a machete.) But in protecting the hawksbill the major problem is not Indian and Toreño butchering for food; destruction of nests is much more significant.Though their collection is illegal, hawksbill eggs sold openly at the Bocas market in July 1979 for fifty cents a dozen. Indian population is increasing near beaches and Guaymí and Toreños here agreed that only a small part of the nests made by hawksbill along this entire coast escaped detection in 1979. Major emphasis should also be placed upon controlling those who buy the shell. The shell's high price is responsible now for a wholesale slaughter of the hawksbills. In the summers of 1978 and 1979, dozens of people were hunting the turtles at night with flashlights. For instance, crews of coastal boats, over-nighting in local havens, even gave up their sleep to go out looking for them. Casa Union, a general merchandising company in Colón, is said to be the principal buyer of the shell.

The green turtle is hardier in captivity than is the hawksbill. It is more strictly vegetarian and can be penned and fed with hibiscus and mangrove leaves, or with sea grass. The hawksbill needs a more varied diet. Many hawksbill die on boats carrying them to market. The turtles continue to lay eggs while on the boat, since few have completed spawning before being captured. The male hawksbill is especially fragile; as Jamaican-English speakers in Bocas say, it "frets, gets cross" and dies sooner when transported.

The leatherback, or trunk, turtle does not enter Almirante Bay or Chiriquí Lagoon, keeping rather to beaches facing the open sea. It arrives here before the other three species, adults being present mainly between March and May; they are rarely seen in June. The eggs hatch in May and June, a month or so before those of the hawksbill. It is the largest of all turtles, so big that boys sometimes ride one down the beach. Leatherback turtle eggs are almost as large as an orange, while the eggs of the others look something like wrinkled ping-pong balls. The Guaymí eat leatherback turtle eggs, but the flesh is not eaten; in fact, elsewhere, the flesh has been reported to be poisonous. I found five nests dug up by egg collectors on the beach within a mile of the Río San Pedro in 1979.

The loggerhead, too, lays its eggs on these beaches. Its flesh is described as being "very rank," especially the fat—but it is occasionally eaten. The loggerhead is somewhat larger than the hawksbill, about the same size as the greenback. It is said to be bad-tempered, the "crossest" of all the turtles.

Thus, since the hawksbill, leatherback turtle, and loggerhead all lay their eggs on this coast, residents of the Province claim they have three "native" turtles. The nests of all three can be found near the mouth of the Río Caña.

The tidal range on the Atlantic coast of Panama is unusually small (less than a meter); and beaches here are but narrow strips, even at low tide. Of all animal

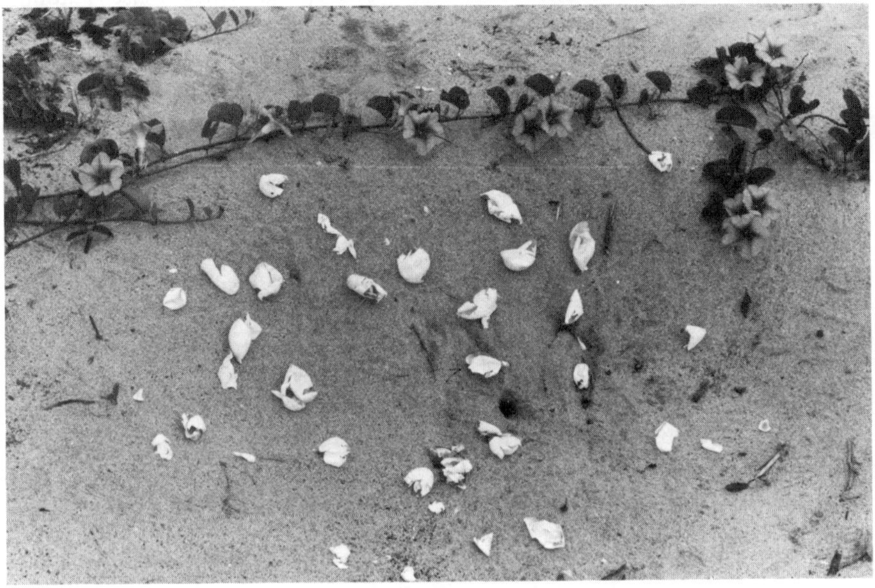

Shells of trunk turtle eggs on the beach near the mouth of the Río San Pedro. The nest was dug up and the eggs eaten by dogs. (The flowering vine, *Ipomea* sp. is a characteristic beach plant. (Below) Hawksbill eggs, next two small bananas for scale. On sale at Bocas market, July, 1979.

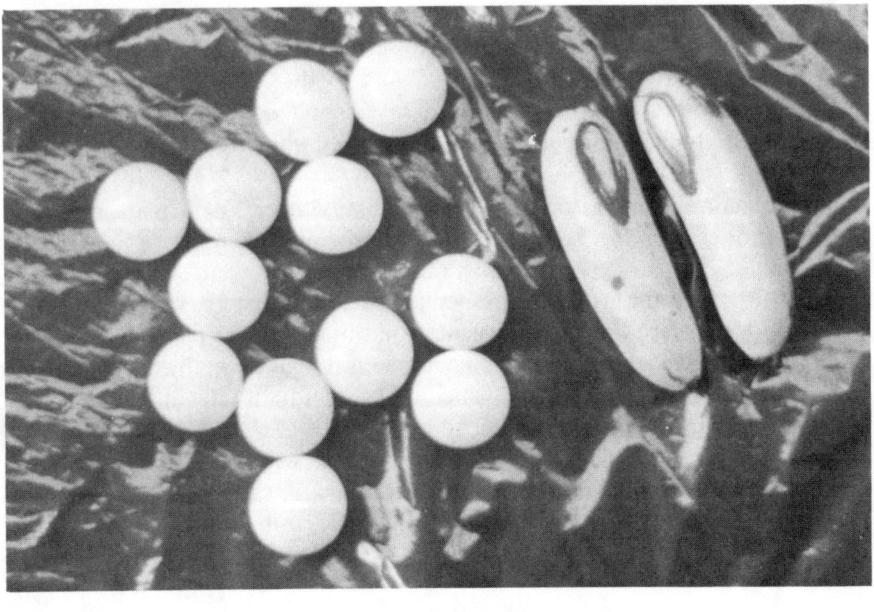

habitats in the area, the beach is the most exposed; and nowhere else is human traffic so heavy. Despite its limited area, this stretch of sand is of special importance to animal life—inland and marine. Both land and sea animals use the beach during a critical stage in their reproductive cycles; for example, the white land crab is independent of the sea, just as the marine turtles are completely independent of the land—except that both must come to this sandy boundary to spawn. Iguanas, too, travel from the wooded banks of inland streams and estuaries to lay their oval eggs in the beach sand; people dig up bagsful for food. Here on the beach, all such animals are especially vulnerable to human predation. (Current proposals for the contruction of a sea level interoceanic canal eastward, in central Panama, pose the possibility of further threat to littoral life in the area).

Though each blames the other, Toreños and Guaymí have jointly fished out almost all large spiny lobsters from shallow parts of the embayment; most were sold to local Chinese for shipment to Colón. The lobster is caught on a short stick with a loop of wire at the end.

In coastal waters the following are the principal Guaymí and Bókata food fishes; all are small:

The *tití* is known to Indians and Bocatoreños alike. The advanced larvae or fry congregate in large schools at the mouths of rivers and streams. While still in the surf the fry have a reddish tinge and turn little patches of the nearshore water pink. Moving from the surf zone into the rivers they are only about an inch long and almost transparent, though within a few days they begin to develop darker pigment. The fry may linger at the mouths of streams for days, staying in deeper water during daylight hours, probably to avoid predators, and moving into the shallows at night. When especially heavy rains fall and the river turns muddy, the fish move upstream (again probably because they are less vulnerable to predators in murky water). Some migrate almost to the headwaters, where they develop dark stripes and reach a length of seven or eight inches. There, the fish is sought by the Indians in the fast- moving waters which it prefers; it clings to rocks with a sucking protuberance on its belly.

But the main *tití* catch is of the fry. The Indians come downstream and catch large quantities with dip nets. (Many other predators congregate there at the same time.) Since *tití* flee from light, they must be netted in semi-darkness.

Some of the fry are boiled for immediate use, but most are roasted or dried. Columbus's son, recalling his experiences on this coast, was probably speaking of this very fish when he wrote, "it is a marvelous thing how many there are at the time when they enter these rivers, which they the Indians take in great quantity and preserve for a long time." (Sauer, 1966, p. 133).

Along the coast most fishing from shore is done with hook and line at river mouths. Immature specimens of all the following were caught by Indian boys in a single evening at the mouth of the Río San Pedro in July, 1979:

English	Spanish	Guaymí	Latin
characin	*sardina*	**dobó**	*Astyanax fasciatus aeneus*
cichlid	*chógara*	**bugó**	*Cichlasoma maculicauda*
jack	*jurél*	**kingí**	*Caranx latus*
left-eyed flounder	*mediopesce*		*Citharichthys arenaceus*
mojarra	*giro*	**tugí**	*Eucinostomus argenteus*
mullet	*liza*		*Agonostomus monticola*
red snapper	*pargo*		*Lutjanus* sp.
sleepers	*guabino*	**udólo**	*Gobiomorus dormitator*

Such marine species as the red snapper, grunt, and jack grow to a good size: red snapper may weigh as much as ten pounds and the jack even more. These, and barracuda, are also caught within Almirante Bay and Chiriquí Lagoon. Kingfish and tarpon are usually caught near offshore coral reefs. However, smaller fish are more important as food, being taken daily and in larger numbers; for instance, the mojarra, the cichlids, and young left-eyed flounders caught in the surf at the river mouths; and sleepers and mullets, taken somewhat farther into the river.

Several fish species, e.g. the califeva (a gray mullet), are especially common in brackish estuaries, and shrimp, particularly the **kebe** (*Macrobrachium acanthurus*) are numerous near the large patches of *caño*-grass which grow there. *Caño*-grass was an important food for the manatee, once plentiful hereabouts but virtually extinct now. Manatees were seen around Bocas del Toro by the 17th century buccaneer and explorer Dampier, who described them in detail. The animal survived in Almirante Bay and Chiriquí Lagoon into the present century (Goldman, 1920, p. 69).

The products of several plants may also be listed among coastal resources. Mangrove wood is a useful fuel, burning (though poorly) when freshly cut. These days it is much used for making charcoal. The seagrape (widespread on Caribbean beaches and unrelated to the grapes of higher latitudes) is one of the more important wild fruit trees in the area.

A tall shrub, the cocoplum, grows with the sea grape at the inner edge of the beach. The fruit ripens in January but since the plants are bearing flowers, as well as the ripe fruit, it probably fruits again within a couple of months. There are two varieties, both ripening at the same time. One has red fruits, one white. The "plums" are sweetish, but astringent, with a rather cottony texture. Cocoplum Point is named for the plant. The fruit of the *sol-sol,* another beach shrub, is also edible.

Intermixed at shoreline with sea grape and cocoplum, and extending in a thin line along the inland edge of mangrove swamps, is a small hibiscus tree, the maho, with beautiful varicolored flowers; its bast is used for making rough cordage.

Coconuts grow along much of the sandy shoreline. For most of the coast the nuts are now the principal vegetable export. But the coconut is only marginally an Indian resource, since Bocatoreños now own virtually all of the trees.

The califéva, a large mullet—probably a variety of the common gray mullet—is found in the brackish water of barrier-beach estuaries where it feeds in patches of aquatic plants growing the shallow water. Guaymí and Toreños spear the fish, since it will not take a hook. A jack and two small barracuda (with brain coral) caught by Guaymí settlers at San Cristobal Island in Almirante Bay.

The product and its container (produced in Japan, distributed from San Francisco) were gathered from the ends of the earth. Its arrival here completes a series of exercises in needless energy consumption: A Japanese fishing fleet, powered by oil from a distant desert; scrap iron, shipped to the Orient to make cans; wood pulped in northern forests for the paper; a freighter to San Francisco, and another to Panama; a two day journey by coastal launch from Colón; and delivery by canoe through a heavy surf to be sold in a fisherman's paradise, to a born fisherman. The product arrived with several other tokens of economic progress now well-established in tropical hinterlands—three boxes of carbonated soft drinks and a carton of soda crackers.

The store owner was outraged, but not by the waste in transport: This particular brand is new here, and the puzzled Guaymí had expressed misgivings about the relationship of the can's contents to the mermaid on the label.

10

COMMERCIAL AGRICULTURE

COMMERCE BETWEEN the Atlantic and Pacific coasts of Panama is almost limited to the neighborhood of the Canal, where one may cross the Isthmus by boat, train, or auto. Elsewhere, no roadway connects the two coasts, and there is little transport except by air. Old trails across the Isthmus are less used now than they were before the Canal was built.

Commercial traffic to the trade centers of Bocas del Toro Province is by water along the coast from Colón, or by air. Separated from other Panamanians by rugged, almost impassable forested country, people of the Province often complain of their isolation. A commonly heard opinion is that the interests of the Province are of but slight concern to the Government of Panama. The building of a road over the mountains to join the towns of Chiriquí Province with Almirante has been discussed for a long time. The road is far from being finished, though this is perhaps all to the good in terms of the survival of native cultures; isolation and impenetrability have made the area something of an Indian refuge from Conquest time to the present.

The town of Bocas del Toro is the site of one of the United Fruit Company's oldest stations, established at the beginning of this century. The Chiriquí Land Company (its local name) later moved its headquarters to Almirante on the mainland. In recent years Changuinola has become its main center of activity. The Company's banana plantations lie between Almirante and the Costa Rican border, especially on the floodplains of the lower Changuinola, San San, and Sixaola rivers. Groves of raphia palm in the swampier parts of the Company land between Changuinola and Sixaola, were at first avoided in laying out banana farms, but many have now been cleared and the ground drained.

In the first decade of this century, business interests in the Province were diverse. During its formative years the Company had a half dozen rivals in the Province; but this diversity has long since disappeared and the banana growing activity of the Company is the basic economic factor in the Province. Most other industries are service industries; for example, the local cattle industry simply provides meat for Company towns.

Between 1939 and 1953, banana diseases had a devastating effect on banana plantations, and thus upon all commerce in the Province. During this time some abacá was grown; though related to the banana, it is immune to Sigatoka and Panama diseases. During this time cacao and rice growing were secondary ventures, and the Company operated a large cattle ranch on Chiriquí Lagoon. In 1953, after some control over the banana diseases had been established, the first banana shipment since 1939 left Almirante. Abacá and rice production were given up; cacao planting was cut back; and within a short time, at the Panamanian Government's insistence, the Company divested itself of its cattle growing properties.

The whole area has been affected by the renewal of Company activities. A series of banana varieties have been grown in an attempt to reduce susceptibility to disease and to reduce wind damage. For example, Gros Michel was the variety planted when the revival of banana production began here in 1953, but within a year disease broke out again and it was replaced by a more resistant variety—the Lacatan. Being very tall stemmed, the Lacatan turned out to be susceptible to wind damage and, in 1966, yet another variety, the Valery, replaced it.

Water levels in these flatlands are now carefully adjusted; mineral fertilizers are imported in quantity; crop-dusting aircraft spray the area with insecticides, etc. At present, Company emphasis is almost entirely upon banana production, and commercial agriculture thrives.

The Banana Industry and Urban Guaymí

BECAUSE OF GOVERNMENT curtailment of the immigration of foreign laborers into Panama, the United Fruit Company began hiring large numbers of Guaymí in 1953 and 1954, to work in Almirante and Changuinola. At that time, Company and private launches carried some and a number came in canoes, mainly from the Cricamola Valley. In 1954, as many as 2,900 employees, some 40 percent of the Company's total labor force, was Guaymí. Because the Guaymí tend to drift homeward after making a few dollars the Company began providing living quarters along the railroad tracks between Almirante and Guabito; since that time, many Indians have brought their families, especially to the vicinity of the new towns, Changuinola and Empalme. The banana plantations are subdivided into "farms" and nowadays those Guaymí employees who have wives are given housing in the small settlements associated with each farm.

The Company has had considerable trouble with drunkenness among its Guaymí employees, although they are not habitual drunkards. The drinking begins on payday, and the Indians often lose several days' work around that time. Liquor vendors say that, although the Indian is thought of as a heavy drinker, he actually drinks less than others; his way of celebrating simply makes his drinking conspicuous.

Fighting of some sort is a great Guaymí pastime, and probably accounts for their being known locally as "Valientes." Until several years ago, fist fights between drunken Guaymí were a common sight on the streets of Almirante and Bocas. Each fighter delivers an involved chant before the fight begins, his adversary listening with an air of exaggerated politeness and interest. The chanting sounds something like a beehive to the non-Guaymí, and is remarkable for its length and monotony. When the chant finally breaks off, each begins to pummel the other, saying, often prematurely, **tihaméti-maui** ("thus I whip you").

Around payday, a few could be seen fighting almost anytime, night or day, battering each other unmercifully and only stopping occasionally to sleep for an hour or two on the sidewalks. However, the sport is only among themselves, and outsiders are not molested. When their money is spent, they go home or back to work. As they become more citified, the Guaymí drink and fight less. They are, as yet, rarely involved in local criminal activities. And these days, with their families present, they are a stable element in the population.

The Panamanian government compels those Indians who can be contacted to send their children to school. Some of the Guaymí living close to the Bay, for instance around Punto Valiente, comply by putting the children out as servants among Negro families in Bocas and Almirante, where they attend school. They do not remain permanently, however; when they reach the age of eleven or twelve, their parents call for them. While in Bocas they learn to speak Spanish and English, with the peculiar accent of the Jamaicans. Thus a number of Valiente Guaymí are trilingual. In recent years, the Panamanian Government has established a number of schools along the coast within the Guaymí area itself.

Shortcomings of Monocultural Land Use

ALTHOUGH THE Chiriquí Land Company is now operating very successfully, in the long run certain advantages may be claimed in this area for an economy based upon a more diversified subsistence-type agriculture. The danger of complete crop failure as a result of insect attacks and epidemic plant diseases is reduced in a diversified agriculture, whereas such outbreaks are sometimes devastating to tropical monoculture. Between 1939 and 1953, when banana diseases virtually closed down the Company's operations, the towns of Almirante and Bocas were terribly impoverished. Significantly at that same time, the scattered banana gardens of the Indians were not greatly affected, and the Térraba sold bananas along the Company railroad for shipment to Panama throughout the time when the diseases were at their worst.

Regarding insect pests and commercial crops, one of the costliest here is the leafcutter ant (*Atta*). When Toreño owners attempt to grow cash crops on the islands the plants are often destroyed by ants. (Pineapples are a favorite crop on Isla Colón because the ants do not attack them.) Ant depredations are reduced with varying degrees of success by pumping poisonous gases into their deep subterranean nests, by blasting them with dynamite, or by laboriously excavating the nests.

The great destruction done by present-day ants is of considerable interest because islands along this coast are described in historical documents as productive and well peopled (and this despite the fact that island soils, often derived from coralline rock, are less fertile than those on the mainland); for instance Bastimentos Island means "Provision Island." One wonders how the leafcutters were controlled in those times. Here again, the explanation probably lies in the

A leaf-cutter ant carrying a fragment of leaf cut from a shrub. See also p. 100). Panama. (R. Buchsbaum)

varied nature of Indian agriculture. It has long been known that species-rich, undisturbed forests are an unsuitable environment for insect plagues—in contrast to plantations (Schneider, 1939). Unlike the great variety which was found in aboriginal gardens on these islands, only a few crop plants are grown in modern fields, and these receive the nearly undivided attention of *Atta.* For some reason the ants are more destructive on the islands than on the mainland. Again this may be because on the islands crop plants are, in places, one of the few foods available to them—as a result of the more complete removal of wild-growing plants there.

Cacao growing represents one of the few adaptations of the old Indian tree garden to modern commercial production, and it has certain merits over other kinds of monoculture. Indians in Central America long ago learned the advantage of growing cacao under tall leguminous (i.e. nitrogen-fixing) shade trees. Among the trees commonly used are various species of *Inga;* e.g. the Térraba make much use of the huge-fruited *guavo* and other trees of the legume family such as *almendro. Mataratón* was used for this purpose in prehistoric Central America; it is still known by the name *madre de cacao* ("mother of chocolate") in some areas.

Cacao orchards are long-lived; many are kept cleared of invading trees and undergrowth only when there is sufficient demand for cacao beans. Orchards which have been abandoned for years may be renewed and harvested when prices are high. Ecologically, cacao is the least disruptive of commercial crops since in cacao-culture a tree cover of several species is maintained, and the orchards support some undergrowth and an associated animal life, at least. Nevertheless, grown as a single crop in large plantations cacao is, like the banana, occasionally damaged by epidemics—particularly witches-broom disease.

Pumpkin River is one of the larger cacao-producing districts. Bucatoreño families near the shores of Chiriquí Lagoon have numerous small orchards. A company called Baker Chocolate Company once had a large plantation in Guaymí territory near Cocoplum Point, and Guaymí families who live in that neighborhood have adopted the name "Baker."

Although seasonal weather fluctuations are not pronounced here, they occasionally occur. If bad weather causes the failure of a crop, the economic effect is not drastic if that crop is only one of many. The high winds which cause devastating "blow downs" on the banana plantations are less destructive in the landscape of forest, thicket, and small clearings associated with Indian land use. Advantages more specifically economic could be claimed for diversification; the greater the variety of local resources, the more feasible it is to satisfy needs locally, and the less the overall waste in transporting goods and people.

The Cattle Industry and Grasslands: Ecological Effects

UNDER NATURAL CONDITIONS, that is before human disturbance, rainforest extended from Yucatan southeastward around the Caribbean to the vicinity of the Magdalena River in Colombia. Toward the ends of this forested area, where climate becomes progressively drier and has an increasingly pronounced rainless season, broad areas of rainforest already had been cleared in prehistoric times, producing grass-covered surfaces known as "savannas." Thus, production of grassland at the expense of forest is an old practice. In places, for instance in northern Colombia, tropical forests showed strong recuperative powers, reforestation of cleared areas occurring in times of diminished landuse. (Gordon, 1957). Nevertheless, where large tracts of forest are involved biotic variety is doubtless lost in each cycle of destruction and renewal. And it must be admitted that such losses probably occur even when deforestation is incomplete, as is the case with Guaymí landuse.

The problem of savanna formation was critical for the Mayas in the northern part of Yucatan where the climate is seasonally dry. As Mayan clearings there were enlarged and extended to the margins of neighboring savannas, they were invaded by grasses, the bane of the pre-European agriculturist. Grassland was extremely difficult to till, and the grasses stifled gardens. (In prehistoric times there were no domesticated gramivores in the American tropics and it was after the introduction of cattle by Europeans that most intensive use was made of savanna areas.) Savanna encroachment has been suggested as a cause of the Mayan decline in northern Yucatan (Morley, 1947, p. 153). On the other hand, extension of savannas can hardly have caused the depopulation which took place in the Mayan Old Empire of the wetter forests farther south.

The characteristics of regrowth vegetation, in Bocas del Toro Province and the other more humid parts of Central America, may throw some light on the causes of Mayan decline. It seems likely that the Mayan food supply was based less completely upon maize cultivation and agriculture per se than is commonly supposed (Lundell, 1933, p. 73), and that over much of the Mayan territory, as in large parts of Bocas del Toro Province, arboriculture and agriculture went hand in hand. Preservation of a varied plant cover similar to the original forest may partially explain the centuries of high yields in the Mayan area. The limestone soils there are prone to quick depletion and erosion when completely exposed, and especially so under repeated plantings of a single crop such as maize. If loss of control over the environment was a cause of depopulation in southern Yucatan, rather than resulting from the incursion of savannas, it may have come about when social disorganization permitted carefully selected and controlled forest and regrowth vegetation there to deteriorate into weedy tangle, and to run rampant with all its natural vigor. Where this occurs, land reclamation is no doubt difficult. In the case of the Maya, the social disorganization may have arisen internally, whereas for the Indians of Bocas del Toro Province, as with the Zenú and Coiba-Cueva peoples, it followed the Spanish conquest.

The raising of beef cattle has been one of the most successful forms of commercial landuse in the American tropics, and a drastic reduction in the total area of rainforest is in progress. As noted above, it is around the margins of the forest, in climates with a pronounced dry season, that replacement of forest by grass is easiest. The farther the grass cover is extended into wet interior portions of the forest, the more expensive its maintenance becomes. Whereas cattle raising is widespread on the Pacific slopes of western Panama, in Bocas del Toro Province, which lacks a rainless season, the cattle industry has been important only during the last few decades; large pastures are as yet found only in lowlands and on coastal hills. But despite the fact that Bocas del Toro Province as a whole appears to be climatically beyond the limits of a profitable cattle industry, and though much of its terrain is rough, pastures continue to expand at the expense of forest because of the great local demand for beef in growing Company towns.

There are a number of cattle ranches along the Río Changuinola, not far from the banana plantations. At Miramar and Chiriquí Grande on Chiriquí Lagoon cattlemen have cleared large tracts of forest, and at times as many as a hundred *macheteros,* most of them Guaymí, find employment there. Bocatoreños have made small pastures on the islands in Almirante Bay, and many archaeological sites which were covered by heavy forest ten years ago are now being grazed by cattle. New pastures are appearing along the coast and being extended inland along river banks, even in the eastern part of the Province; a number of Guaymí families there have, themselves, begun to grow cattle for shipment to Almirante and Bocas. The cattle industry extends farther eastward each year, and one can readily follow the progress of ecological change at the forefront of pasture-making.

The most conspicuous ecological changes associated with the cattle industry are, of course, the elimination of the forest itself and the introduction of forage grasses (mainly perennials of African origin) and associated pasture weeds. In making pastures, all woody vegetation is cleared away except for an occasional shade tree. Without the machete it would be impossible to maintain such pastures in this humid climate. They must be frequently "cleaned" (the Spanish verb "limpiar" is used) of regrowth—machete wielders slashing almost any shrubs or tree seedlings that reappear.

Around Bocas and eastward along the coast in the Guaymí area four of the more common introduced forage grasses are *zacote,* elephant grass, *jaragua* and, especially in newly-made pastures, *pará.*

Cosmopolitan weeds arrive with the pasture grasses. One of the worst from the cattleman's standpoint is the sensitive plant, known locally as "shame weed." Lantana and vervain are also common. A small leguminous shrub called *pega-pega* quickly becomes abundant where pasture is made. The plant's fruits are flat, jointed pods, covered with minute hooked hairs; these stick to the skins of cattle, and the plant spreads wherever cattle go. Although *pega-pega* is something of a nuisance because its pods are also adhesive to clothing, it is generally favored by cattlemen; it is said to have considerable forage value.

Pasture on recently cleared forest land. Zebu cattle and cattle egrets. The egret is of African origin as are most of the pasture grasses upon which the cattle feed.

The *guázumo* tree often appears in pastures, where it is left standing for cattle shade. *Mataratón* is commonly planted as living fence posts upon which to string barbwire. The balsam apple, an orange-fruited vine, and jackass bitters, a shrub, are common around the margins of pastures.

A number of animal species extend their range with the pastures, for example the ani, a black native bird widely known in the Caribbean area for its association with the cattle industry, and the African cattle egret. Both birds promptly appear as new pastures are made, e.g. in those recently made near the mouth of the Río San Pedro. Another notorious associate of cattle grasses here is a tiny red chigger called *coloradito,* which produces red welts on the human skin and an exasperating itching.

The white-tailed deer, and probably various other savanna animals, have periodically entered and left this area over the centuries as the forest cover was thinned or cleared, and then reestablished itself. Absent from unbroken forest, the deer favors areas of mixed herbaceous cover and regrowth thickets. It has recently spread eastward from Costa Rica through newly-made pastures and can now be found around Almirante Bay.

The great-tailed grackle, though not especially associated with cattle, also extends its range here following deforestation; it favors shoreline villages and coconut trees. The grackle arrived in Bocas from Costa Rica around 1969, and in the last few years has spread rapidly eastward. Nowadays, conspicuous in Bocas and Almirante, it squabbles for perching space with crimson-fronted parakeets as the latter arrive evenings to roost in palm trees planted there. Townspeople describe the grackle as a nuisance, saying that it steals rice and corn put out to dry. Noisy and active throughout the day—constantly preening itself, scolding and posturing (e.g., pointing its bill upward), the grackle now outdoes the kiskadee in disturbing the town's quiet afternoons. Spreading from hamlet to hamlet around Chiriquí Lagoon and eastward along the coast, the grackle has reached the Río San Pedro only recently—late in 1977; there it is known as "the Bocas bird," having come from the direction of that town.

Great-tailed grackle—a newcomer, unknown here a few years ago (Ridgely, 1976, p. 309).

Around Almirante Bay several small birds, "grass birds" as they are called hereabouts, are especially numerous along the edges of the pastures where forage grasses escape grazing and go to seed—for example, the white-collared seedeater, the black seedeater, and the variable seedeater. These birds are not found in the forest and rarely in Guaymí clearings (except where rice is grown), but are common nearby in coastal pastures. Birds which spread with grassland here include not only the seedeaters but insectivores, as well: for example, the social flycatcher, the common tody flycatcher, and the long-tailed tyrant. The latter is now found around pastures on the lower Río San Pedro.

Aside from pasture grasses, the great influx of Old World weeds which is so typical of old fields in mid-latitude America has not occurred here. Away from the coast and the cattle industry few alien weeds grow in Bokatá and Guaymí clearings; there grasses, native or otherwise, form a small part of the herbaceous vegetation.

The extensive clearing of forests which is underway in tropical America is, with good reason, of grave concern to conservationists; numerous plant and animal species are threatened. The author collected some 250 species from a small area in eastern Bocas del Toro Province; of these, six were identified by expert taxonomists as possibly new. Certainly as the total area of American rainforests is diminished, in addition to known exterminations, large numbers of undescribed species are disappearing as well. The tropical biomass is probably the planet's richest remaining storehouse of naturally-occurring organic compounds. The names of all valuable organic compounds and products discovered in the American tropics would make a lengthy list indeed (e.g. coumarin, curare, quinine, rubber, etc.); most were first made known to us by Indian inhabitants themselves. Uses (including medicinal uses) for many more will probably be discovered, barring their complete destruction as a result of deforestation.

11

CULTURAL, TERRITORIAL AND DEMOGRAPHIC CHANGES

DURING AN EARLIER PERIOD, human populations lived in a state of since-unrivalled intimacy with the plant and animal world, domesticating during that time most of the species upon which modern agriculture is based. No doubt the processes of domestication were sped during this biotechnic era, when entire populations gave special consideration to the qualities of plants and animals.

In western Panama the Guaymí and others—subsisting directly from forest and garden—continue a similar relationship with nature, and the landscape has been transformed accordingly: Animal habitats range through a series of more or less modified plant associations; from undisturbed forest, through all stages of regrowth, to tree gardens and maize plots. And plant species themselves range from the strictly wild, through forms which have been more or less altered taxonomically by their associations with people, to the domesticated.

However, since European settlement began here and commercial agriculture has developed, these Indians' ties with nature have weakened. As in many other areas of declining native cultures, subtle beginnings of domestication have been cut short, and even well-developed domesticated forms are disappearing: The old accounts, cited above, which describe the Indians' raising of young tapirs and being followed about by tame peccaries are evidence of once closer relationships with forest mammals; the wax insect, axin, at one time widely propagated has almost disappeared here, as in Mexico; stingless bees are now rarely kept; a distinctive variety of Guaymí maize, sown rather than planted, is now seldom grown; the Térraba's smooth-fruited *pataste* is becoming rare; the special variety of wild pineapple which is widely cultivated by the Guaymí for its superior fibers will itself probably be given up if the recently-begun trade in nylon continues; etc. Similarly, in the Sunú area of Columbia a cultivated variety of the wild cane is grown only by a few surviving Indians.

With regard to changing man-land relationships, aside from those relatively small areas where regrowth is a consequence of natural disturbance, two general types of *rastrojo* are distinguishable today: One type, selected and controlled, has been described above; it is now of limited extent, being found only around Indian communities and in rural Spanish-speaking areas where Indian influences are strong (Gordon, 1957, p. 84-86). Probably most of the trees now grown in Indian gardens (papaya, *membrillo,* monkey head, *pataste* etc.) had their beginnings in prehistoric regrowth of this type, where their stictly wild ancestors were subjected to just such selective pressures as those still exerted by the Guaymí.

The other type of regrowth is, by contrast, an unsorted and generally unused tangle: It covers great areas; for example, where commercial lumbering operations have taken place and where pastures are overgrown; cattlemen view *rastrojo* as a relentless and costly nuisance. Similarly, on Company banana plantations such vegetation provides nothing of value, and is only visited by machete-wielding employees when the land it covers is needed.

Indian Acculturation

The order in which traits are lost in the acculturation process varies almost unpredictably. In one culture, religion may collapse first; in another, native language or political organization. But in the forests of Isthmian America, agricultural features such as domesticated plants, their names and their uses, outlive most other cultural traits. For instance, the Christian, Spanish-speaking Cholos along the Veraguas border, like the Hispanicized descendants of the Zenu in Colombia, practice an agriculture which is in large part pre-Columbian in character. To be sure, Guaymí in the savannas on the Pacific slope have lost much of their horticultural tradition, many having become cattle-raisers; but here physical environment is probably the determining factor.

Further on the subject of acculturation sequences, it is interesting to compare the Térraba with the Guaymí Indians and the Cholos. The latter are almost purely of Indian descent but stoutly proclaim themselves to be Spanish. Although they do not speak an Indian language, much that is Indian may be observed among them, particularly their artifacts. The Térraba are no less modified racially, but refer to themselves as Indians and, as noted, retain their native language; yet they have considerably less of the aboriginal in their material culture than have the Cholos.

The Térraba are in some ways linguistically conservative: in speaking their own language they generally do not use foreign names for introduced objects. For instance, *shuáng* is clothing in general; *zukra* is knife; thus, scissors have become *shuang-zukra.* Matches are called *yókra.* There are but few exceptions, e.g. the Spanish words *naranja* (orange) and *arroz* (rice) and the English word *soap*. Similarly, when speaking Spanish, they rarely mix in Térraba terms. The Guaymí, on the other hand, although they are generally less acculturated than the Térraba, readily incorporate foreign terms into their language, giving the words a peculiar pronunciation which makes them hard to recognize. Examples are *majĩ* for English matches; and *zabada* for the Spanish *zapato* (shoe).

As noted above, the Indians of Bocas del Toro Province acquired the machete and the pig at an early date. The importance attained by some of these old introduced traits can be seen in the fact that they now even play a part in Guaymí burial custom: when an inland Guaymí dies he is buried beneath his house with his machete and occasionally (even these days, I was told) with a slain pig, or chicken. The house is then abandoned. Coastal Guaymí now follow Christian burial custom.

Another instance of conservatism: some old European customs are preserved in Central America by Indian people only. For instance, the last Térraba chief confined tribal criminals in stocks, and Guaymí chiefs have done so within the last few years—the stocks being known among both groups by the Spanish name *cepo*. (I have read that certain Mexican Indians, e.g. the Huichol, recently did the same.)

But the general trend has been toward loss of distinctive cultural traits: for instance, metal cooking utensils are bought, almost no pottery having been made in the last few decades except in remote neighborhoods such as the upper Río Caña. Salt is now bought, though old Bocatorenos can remember when the Guaymí made salt by boiling sea water. Aniline has replaced many of the vegetable dyes. Kerosene has long been a trade item replacing local vegetable oils. In recent years, shops and schools have been established along the coast, the former selling canned goods, soft drinks, etc. Lately nylon cord, smuggled out of Company storehouses at Changuinola and sold to the Guaymí, is being used by some Guaymí in place of wild pineapple fibers for making carrying bags. And Guaymí returning home from Almirante occasionally bring transistor radios.

Indian clothing style has greatly changed. The earliest report notes that "all go naked along this coast except for their private parts, which the women and the men cover with *cloth they get from the inner bark of trees*." (Sauer, 1966, p. 131). Nevertheless, early accounts also record a knowledge of weaving here though apparently little use was made of cotton clothing. Small Guaymí children still go about in bark loincloths; and women wear the same sort of loincloth under cotton dresses.

About twenty-five years ago, when I first visited the area, some Bókata women still made their clothing entirely of bark cloth, and in the same style of voluminous "mother hubbard" favored by Guaymí women who buy cloth from traders. Both the Guaymí and almost all Bókata women now use printed cotton trade cloth. (The style, itself, is an old Spanish influence.) Bark cloth is actually not a very satisfactory material for such expansive clothing, being thick, stiff, easily shredded, and difficult to wash: The Bókata women often washed such dresses without removing them, by standing at the streamside and scrubbing the cloth with a piece of soft bark dipped in water. During those times, too, Bókata wore bulky necklaces with numerous strings; the beads were the light blue seeds of Job's tears (an African plant, supposedly introduced here in post-Colombian times) which grows along the lower courses of some of the rivers. Both Bókata and Guaymí girls still commonly wear smaller necklaces made of the brilliantly red and black seeds of a leguminous forest tree (*Ormosia?*).

Missionary activities are now stronger than ever. Here on the Atlantic slope those Indians who profess Christianity are mostly Protestants. For example, Wesleyan Methodists have a mission at Cusapín, and the Seventh-day Adventists have meetings on the Río Chiriquí. But the Roman Catholics have also established a mission at Canquintu on the lower Río Cricamola. On the Pacific slope the efforts of Catholic missionaries have been more or less continuous since the Conquest. Nevertheless, missionaries of other sects are active there, too. In recent years, some missionaries have, fortunately, somewhat de-emphasized the need for cultural change among the Guaymí.

Guaymí hunting pressure is partly compensated for by their land use practices, which make many animals more abundant than they would be under strictly natural conditions. Traditional hunting methods appear to pose little threat to the survival of native animal species. (A possible exception, often pointed to by other Panamanians, is the Guaymí use of fish poisoning plants.)

On the other hand, various introduced hunting implements are beginning to have significant destructive effects. For example, many Guaymí have long had small-calibre rifles, which are no doubt responsible for the severely reduced populations of tapir and jaguar. Flashlights and underwater gear pose a further threat, especially in the hands of such skilled hunters as these. Along the coast some Guaymí now use flashlights and guns for night hunting, particularly for the paca which, being nocturnal, is hard to kill without them; it is temporarily blinded by light. Another example: One evening two boys borrowed my flashlight for night hunting. When they returned they carried a rufous-tailed hummingbird and a great kiskadee for roasting; both birds, blinded by light, were snatched from perches on tree limbs. Fortunately flashlight batteries are costly in Guaymí country and don't last long in this climate. (Around Almirante Bay and northern Chiriquí Lagoon, outside Guaymí country, where headlamps and guns are more readily available, many nocturnal animals have been almost hunted out.) In the few places where the Guaymí have acquired flippers, underwater goggles and spring-spears, iguanas have almost disappeared: The iguanas are speared underwater after they have leapt into the river from the branches of streamside trees; before this gear was introduced the iguana was protected by its ability to remain submerged for some time. But all such threats to wildlife are as nothing compared to that posed by the clearing of forests for the expanding cattle industry.

Expansion of Guaymí Territory

THE GUAYMI are increasing in number rapidly and extending their territory around Chiriquí Lagoon and Almirante Bay. In 1953, when I first visited this area, Guaymí lived along the south end of Chiriquí Lagoon no farther westward than a spot called Chiriquí Grande, although an area beyond this point was then incorrectly shown on some maps as already within their territory. The northwest boundary of Guaymí territory lay near the Guarumo River, at that time the site of a Company cattle ranch. The forested country to the northwest, from the Río Guarumo to the Río Changuinola, was uninhabited. In 1958, a few Guaymí squatters had settled in the forest on the peninsula separating Almirante Bay and Chiriquí Lagoon. By 1966, several families were living on Isla Popa and Coco Key, and others were occupying parts of the forest west of the Bay—most of which is probably former territory of the extinct Dorasque tribe.

To the southeast of Chiriquicito, Guaymí houses were mainly back from the coast and most numerous in the Guariviara River Valley.

The lower Cricamola Valley was a major Guaymí center in early historic times, but in the last half of the 19th century it was settled by outsiders. A French writer who ascended the Cricamola River in 1883, encountered the first habitations of Valiente Indians at Gobrante (Pinart, 1885, p. 3). At the beginning of this century, the United Fruit Company bought up land in the lower Valley, including the holdings of several independent German fruit growers. The Company quit working this land, however, about 1910, at which time there were few Indians below Baker-tibi (near Canquinto). Until recently, much of the lower part of the valley was still claimed by the Company. At the time when the Company was using its land in the Cricamola Valley, Jamaican Negro employees of the Company occupied farms along the lower river. Most of these Jamaicans left when Company activities terminated, but in 1966, a couple of families and a German farmer remained working land and trading with the Guaymí. About a dozen Indian families were settled below Canquinto, some on Company land, including a family on each side of the river mouth. All had come down river within the previous fifteen or twenty years. They were planting maize along the river and had cleared the raphia palm from a few patches of swampland for rice growing. Throughout all this time until the present, the Guaymí maintained their hold on Valiente Peninsula.

During the last fifteen years, Guaymí expansion westward has been spectacular: Many have settled in the lower Cricamola Valley. Isolated houses are now scattered around the entire western side of the embayment, and the Indians are settling long-undisturbed inland forests west of the Lagoon. On the islands wherever there are unused tracts of forest, they have appeared, asking no one's permission. About a hundred now live on Pope's Island; about 60 on Crawl Cay; and 30 on Salt Creek Island. Generally their dwellings are well separated, but on Isla Cristobal there is a hamlet of nearly a hundred. There are twenty or so on Nancy Key and several families on Isla Colón itself. Northward from Almirante they are beginning to occupy parts of the forest on either side of the railroad, to be nearer relatives among the several thousand Indians who work for the Company around Changuinola. Along the eastern coast of the Province, concentrations of Indians have grown and hamlets developed wherever the Panamanian Government has established schools.

Traditionalist and Separatist Sentiment

IN 1953 the Guaymí seemed to have little interest in Panamanian politics, but by 1956 Indians on both the Pacific and Atlantic slopes of the *serranía* were attending *juntas* (get-togethers) to hear leaders lay claim to land occupied by

Spanish-speaking Panamanians. Nowadays Guaymí land claims are a major political issue in Bocas del Toro Province.

A local religious movement, the Mama-chi cult, has had considerable influence upon Guaymí culture within the last two decades.

Mama-chi was a young Guaymí seeress from the savannas who took up residence in the Cricamola Valley. Her cult was much influenced by Guaymí contacts with Roman Catholic and Seventh Day Adventist missions: For example, Mama-chi had seen Christ in a vision; "sisters" of the cult wear white habits like Catholic nuns, the cross is a principal symbol, etc. In short, the cult is highly syncretic, even expressing certain feminist views. Drunkenness, fighting, polygamy and stick-games are all condemned. Guaymí in the western part of the Province have held no stick-games since 1963; Mama-chi is said to have been concerned with the numerous injuries suffered by contestants, and by the fact that wives were sometimes bet on the outcome.

Despite its condemnation of various old Guaymí customs, the Mama-chi cult generally stimulated traditionalist and separatist sentiment within the tribe. Mama-chi decried Indian intermarriage with whites, blacks, and mestizos, and strongly supported a movement to form an Indian reservation (*Reserva Indigena*). She decried, too, the raising of cattle, the use of barbwire and corrugated iron roofs (all strongly identified in the Guaymí mind with non-Indians).

Mama-chi died in 1965 while still in her early twenties, apparently of tuberculosis. Her cult, which now has its headquarters in Cusapín, has declined; but some of its social effects persist. Recently leaders of the cult have asserted that Indian lands should actually include all of Almirante Bay, and that non-Indians there should move out, with the concession that Bocas and the rest of the Isla Colón ought to be left to the Negroes, i.e. the "Natives."

Other Recent Changes Among the Térraba and Guaymí

WHEREAS LITTLE INFORMATION exists on historical changes in the population and customs of the Bókata and Guaymí in the Province, bits of information are available for the Térraba.

In 1898 a European naturalist gathered demographic notes on the tribe and predicted its early extinction:

> Thiel estimated that in 1824 the number of Térrabas in the Diquís Valley [Costa Rica] was 801; and that the *remainder of the tribe on the upper Tariaria* [Río Teribe, Panamá]*; amounted to 250.* In 1883 San Francisco de Térraba [Costa Rica] still had 299 persons, but by 1892, only 231. Finally, in 1873 Gabb counted in 103 Tírub on the upper Tariaria, and when I visited the group in 1898 a very complete census gave 57, of which 38 were adults; there were 14 boys and 5 girls. ... For the most part these live near Brusik in a wild and almost inaccessible area. (Translated from Pittier, 1903, p. 706).

By the time of the First World War the Térraba had evidently experienced a resurgence: In 1953 several old Bocatoreños assured that there were close to a thousand on the Río Teribe in 1915. During the First World War a terrible epidemic of tuberculosis struck the Térrabas, becoming most severe in 1920 and 1921, and killing many, including their chief. Shortly before he died, the chief went to the hospital at Bocas; people in Bocas say that several hundred Indians came with him, bringing their own food and building thatch shelters outside town. Older Térraba express resentment toward the Company because their chief was refused treatment at the Almirante hospital before he went to Bocas. This re-enforced an old dislike of the Company whose activities here are centered in what was once the best land in Térraba territory; Térrabas still refused to seek employment with the Company until around 1970.

I visited the Térraba briefly in 1953, 1956, 1958, and again in 1979, and over this time their fortunes have changed greatly.

Shortly after World War II, a Seventh Day Adventist arrived from Panamá City. He was much liked and made many converts among the Térraba; the Adventist Indians will not smoke tobacco nor eat pork (in fact, they have quit raising pigs).

The Adventists sent a Térraba girl to Panama to train her as a school teacher. Anticipating her return, a number of families moved downriver to Sie-zhík where, at the missionary's suggestion, they built a thatch-roofed school and church, carving the boards with machetes, and planted flowers and fruit trees. Since teachers sent to Indian communities by the Panamanian government were mainly Negroes from the Canal Zone, the Térraba were proud that one of their own people would have this position. When I first visited them, the young woman had but recently returned from Panama and taught at their school for several weeks. Although she still understood the Térraba language, she refused to speak to her people except in Spanish and reproached them for their non-Hispanic customs. (Mestizos taunt the Indians with the story that their ancestors were cannibals—which is probably not true of the 16th century Térraba, although the Indians accept it.) Then, pleading illness, she went to Almirante where she married. A delegation followed her to Almirante to ask her to return, but she said she could no longer tolerate such an "animal existence." Those Térraba who had not favored missionary activities claimed that this was what could be expected in dealing with outsiders, and by 1954, several of the families had moved back upriver.

Acculturation began earlier among the Térraba than among the Guaymí or Bókata. For instance, although potsherds (often of flat-bottomed vessels decorated with potter's stamps) are common in their fields, the Térraba have made no pottery whatever for decades. In 1953, Térraba and Bribri still occasionally used blowguns for killing small birds, but I was able to find none of the implements in 1979. In 1975, the Térraba wore great strings of beads and tatooed and painted their faces and bodies (Gabb, 1975, p. 519), but they no longer do so. In 1953, a few old women still grew tree cotton and wove cotton belts, but now all weaving has ceased. One critical sign of weakening tradition, and the portent of a more modern economic mentality, is the recent practice of a few Térraba of looting their ancestral burial grounds of gold for sale to outsiders; some have transistor radios and can even quote changing gold prices. (On the other hand, the San Blas Indians, who are even more modernized in some respects than the Térraba, still take a dim view of grave looting activity, and I have not seen it among the Guaymí.)

In 1953, my count of the Térraba population was approximately 250; there were almost certainly fewer than 300 in all. The tribe was socially fragmented: There was a Protestant (Seventh Day Adventist) faction, friendly with "Native" Bocatoreños of the same faith; and an isolationist faction upriver, under the influence of the chief and the *sukia*—plainly too many cultural poles for so small a group. Women were intermarrying with outsiders and many were chosing to lose their identity as Térraba.

The chief, whose authority was not then recognized by the Panamanian government, stayed well upstream, a day's travel by canoe. Downriver lived a Bocatoreño appointed by the government to act as a justice of the peace (*corregidor*) to whom Indians who were dissatisfied with the chief's judgements took their disputes. The chief had but little control; several Térraba spoke wistfully of his father who ruled firmly, enforced tribal laws, forbade carrying disputes to the *corregidor,* and thus held the tribe together. The chief is still living, but he is feeble and his son is now the principal authority. He appoints his own police and has his own jailhouse—not that criminal activity is much of a problem.

Tuberculosis plagues the Térraba even now, and has, perhaps, been one cause of their somewhat pessimistic outlook for their future. Nevertheless, since 1953 there has been a remarkable increase in the birth rate and, more importantly, a pronounced decrease in infant mortality. A government medical dispensary has been established among the Térraba, a Protestant mission employs a nurse, and the Company now has a generous policy providing even Indians who are not employees low-cost treatment at a modern clinic at Changuinola.

Another stimulus to Térraba growth has, curiously, come from the Guaymí. In their plans for an "indigenous territory" Guaymí spokesmen often talk of including the Térraba and their valley within this territory. Térraba leaders after considering the recent westward expansion of the Guaymí, their own relatively small tribal population and the fact that some Guaymí have married Térraba women in the last few years, have come to view this Guaymí proposal—probably correctly—as yet another threat to cultural survival. They are attempting to set up an indigenous territory of their own, quite separate from that of the Guaymí. The chief's son, fearing that Government officials mistake the Térraba for only a minor subdivision of the Guaymí tribe, is engaged in a program emphasizing the viability of Térraba culture and its distinctive qualities: He and others are encouraging larger families, youthful marriages, and marriage within the tribe. They are zealously collecting demographic notes. Their estimate which includes the most recently born infants and children of mixed marriages who still speak some Térraba is, as of July 1979, some two thousand.

This represents a dramatic change in population; but it is by no means certain that such growth insures preservation of Térraba culture. In 1969 or 1970, one of the most disastrous floods in the memory of local residents swept away much of the alluvium in the Teribe Valley, exposing long stretches of large, stream-rounded cobble, thus eliminating much of the most productive land and forcing agriculture back onto the valley slopes. At this time many Térraba ended a long-standing policy and sought employment with the Company. Increased cash purchased medical services and other amenities. The narrow Teribe Valley is too small a land base to support a greatly increased population. And the trend among most Térraba is still strongly toward increased adoption of outside custom and dependence upon supplies from Company towns. On the other hand, the Térraba language thrives and will be an important factor in their future, since it is now the only strong bond among them.

The Térraba are yet another example of a people saved from extermination in the biological sense, but as is so commonly the case with the American Indian, at the price of increased loss of cultural identity. Like the Bribri they are fast becoming indistinguishable from their neighbors in terms of material culture, including land use methods; a few have even cleared hillside forests and begun growing cattle.

The more acculturated and literate the Térraba or Guaymí, the less his knowledge of, or interest in, nature. Public education has, as yet, only encouraged this trend. Despite the accumulation of great amounts of information about these rainforests in scientific journals (all of which, by the way, are printed and read elsewhere), among the inhabitants of the area themselves useful knowledge of natural history is no doubt less complete now than it was four centuries ago—and declining rapidly.

The above comments upon an exemplary Guaymí land use by no means imply a recommendation of all Guaymí custom, some of which is unattractive to outsiders—even to members of neighboring tropical American tribes—for example, their brawling. Nor is their custom of filing teeth likely to have general appeal.

Though the Guaymí are very sensitive to unfavorable comment upon their food, it must be admitted that they are not especially cleanly in preparing meals. Yet, if a newcomer refuses an offering he is likely to go hungry thereafter. And Guaymí thresholds of squeamishness are dizzyingly high: their women's custom of pre-chewing some foodstuffs (e.g. peachpalm fruits and maize) in the preparation of fermented beverages discourages even the least finicky of visitors.

Various other customs are irksome to non-Indians: When birds are captured, the Guaymí commonly pluck them of all their feathers while the birds are still living. I have seen this done among the Chocó Indians of Colombia, too, and been puzzled by what seemed an act of unnecessary cruelty. There may, however, be a practical reason for the custom: I was told that live birds can be

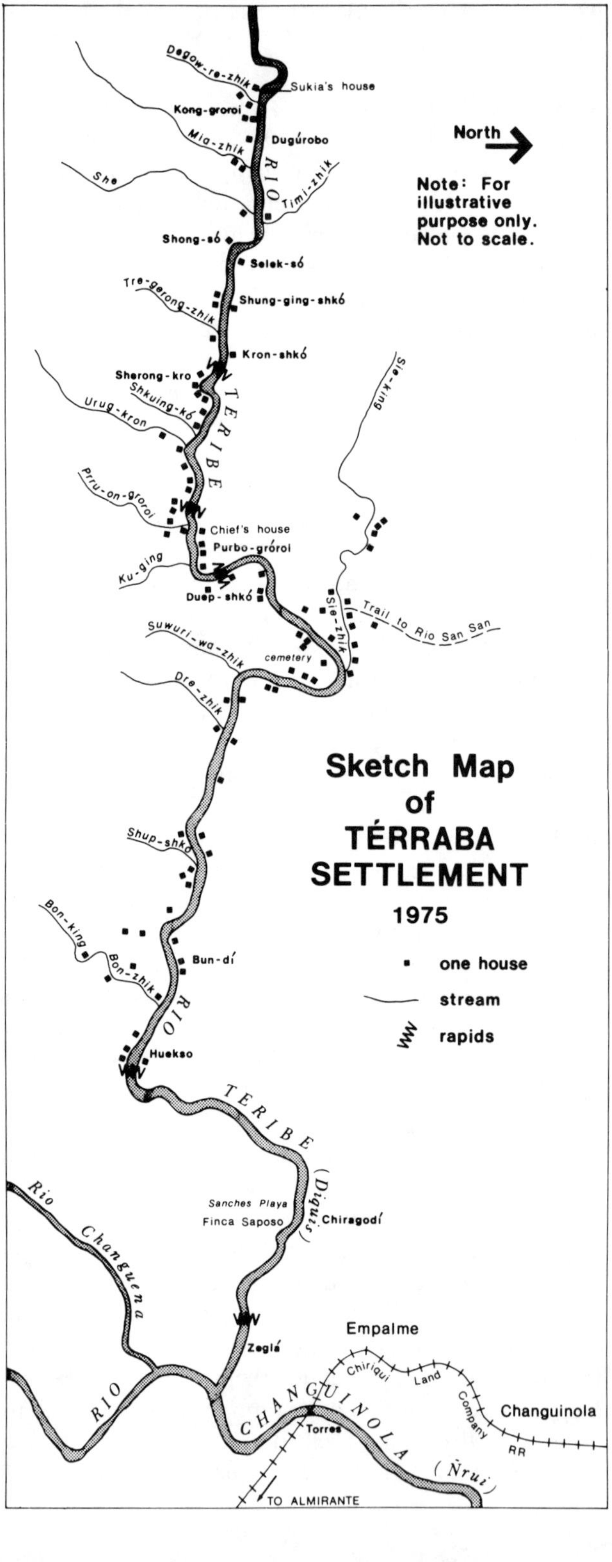

The largest tributaries on the Río Teribe are the Bon, Urúgkron, Mia, She, and the Sie.

The first Indian house encountered in ascending the Río Teribe is at Huek-só as indicated by the suffix *-so,* meaning "Indian"; the suffix also appears in the tribe's name for itself and in the names for neighboring Indian groups.

The chief's house is across from the mouth of the Prru-ongróroi, the word for chief, "prrú," appearing in the streams name. The house of the medicine man, *sukia,* is farther upstream, at Kurú-uo.

The word "kíng" refers to the upper course of a stream, and "zhík" to its mouth; e.g., Bonzhík and Sie-kíng. "Gróroi" means "where there are"; thus, Purbo-groroi means "where there are fruit trees." "Shko" means "the place of"; e.g., Shup-shkó is "the place of the peach palms."

Many places are named for plants and animals: Zegla means "tree fern" (there are many near this spot); Chiragodí is the name of a small palm; Bon is a common fish; Kron is the name for the guava; Shung-gíng is the name for the *guácimo* tree; Urg or Uruk is the name for the tropical cedar, etc.

plucked more easily than can dead birds—without tearing away, and thus wasting, the skin. (To be sure, some of our own practices, e.g. in the plucking and butchering of turkeys, our trimming of the beaks of live chickens, etc. are scarcely more humane).

Despite all this, conservationists interested in protecting these forests would do well to concern themselves with the survival of such native cultures, unattractive though the latter may be in various details.

Compared with other uses of the land in this area (and most definitely so when compared with the cattle industry) the Guaymí system, with its incorporation of human subsistence activities into the rainforest ecosystem, is ecologically benign. Yet when one turns to the Guaymí themselves to learn the system's conceptual basis, next to nothing is heard about such ideas as the need for preserving living resources.

In fact, neighbors of the Guaymí, recently somewhat hardened by contacts with an expanding population of hungry Indians, find the notion that the Guaymí possess knowledge of conservational value, laughable. Instead, the Indian is usually described as a reckless and consummate omnivore, a "walking belly" scouring the countryside for anything living and digestible.

Certainly one will rarely hear the Indians themselves ascribe their land use methods to a special ecological folk wisdom, or even to forethought for some comprehensive long-term advantage. Despite its successes and great potential, their land use system appears to be based upon matter-of-fact tradition (a detailed, but piecemeal, folklore of trial-and-error subsistence practices and yield benefits) rather than upon an overall land use concept, much less a philosophy of conservation.

Are records of such waning native cultures chiefly of antiquarian and nostalgic interest, or can something for the future be learned from the Guaymí and their forests? Recently it has been suggested that good use can be made of the tropical forest biomass by harvesting it for fuel, or by reducing it through chemical processes to cattle fodder. If such proposals are representative of modern thought, Guaymí procedures are, ecologically speaking, indeed ahead of their time.

12

Tropical Silviculture Based Upon Indian Example

OVER THE YEARS these tropics have dealt harshly with a score of utopian schemes. Visionary pronouncements are, understandably, treated with a degree of skepticism. Nevertheless, the picture of a human society thriving in an environment of constantly renewed biotic resources has persistent appeal. As did many of our ancestors, the Guaymí make their living as applied ecologists; and, similarly, they may give up this livelihood for reasons which are partly economic. From the standpoint of the conservationist who thinks in terms of long-term environmental benefits, and who sees the effects of an industry based upon petrochemicals and metals, this seems unfortunate. Even from a strictly economic standpoint, applied ecology as a way of life may have waned before its potential was realized; certainly, before its prospects were fully explored: As world energy resources become more depleted or hoarded, regional self-sufficiency may be increasingly a factor in economic well-being.

The record of Indian settlement shows the value of coercive human action within the forest, rather than destructive action against it. Living within the forest, the Indian settler uses its overwhelming growth potential to his advantage, allowing the reproductive forces of nature to operate for him. A first step in settlement is to increase the number of useful plants by selectively eliminating those for which no uses have been found. The principal change is in relative abundance; no species is exterminated, and the forest canopy remains unbroken. Limited tracts of forest are cleared as agriculture begins; tree-gardens are established, and crops planted.

Picture this, as an example of an enriched ecological setting: widely scattered tall trees form a broken overstorey throughout a dispersed Indian hamlet; the trees rise to a height of roughly 30 m to 45 m; they include *almendro,* breadnut, hog plum, and sapodilly—all of which produce edible fruits.

Intermixed with these is a lower storey of trees about 10 m to 30 m tall: jira palm and *guavos* are among the more common. *Pataste,* peach palm and monkey head are found in the larger openings because they prefer direct sunlight.

Beneath and around these is yet another storey of low-growing trees only 4 m to 10 m tall, e.g. *cacao del monte* and wild cacao growing in well-shaded spots. Achiote, *membrillo* and tree calabash grow both in partial shade and in the sun, while avocado and papaya grow best in direct sunlight. This tree cover is broken by small patches of garden plants mainly rising to a height of less than 4 m. Crops such as bananas, manioc and maize thrive best in sunny spots; otó tolerates both partial shade and sunlight; wild pineapple is grown only in deep shade.

Regrowth plants tend to spread rapidly on untilled plots; the settler allows useful ones to do so. Thus, nearby the gardens and crisscrossed by trails, are numerous patches of productive regrowth in various stages of development. Populations of game animals (for the Indians the term spans most of the animal kingdom) vary throughout, with changing plant cover.

Plants in such settings provide edible fruits, oils, starchy foods, ready fuel, thatch and other building materials, lumber, canoe-logs, fibers, barkcloth, rubber, dyes, medicines, etc. Conditions resembling this which can be seen in tracts of Guaymí, Bókata and Térraba country are rather simple considering those that could exist: a major resource of the forest lies in its organic diversity which makes countless choices and combinations possible.

Despite its merits, the Indian system of forest use can, no doubt, be greatly improved by application of more scientific and systematic methods, and by Guaymí adoption of an educational program designed to build upon their existing knowledge and skills. Plainly, increased literacy with, for example, permanent written records of land use changes would be beneficial.

In attempting to combine maximum diversity with maximum productivity much of the original forest structure must be preserved. Trees can be selected to form a proper canopy for regulating the amount of sunlight penetrating to lower levels. Probably the canopy will have a richer mixture of deciduous species than exists under natural conditions. Deep-rooted, sizable trees which rapidly replenish mineral nutrients to the topsoil, (e.g. trees whose root draw most heavily on minerals dissolving from rocks weathering at depths, and nitrogen-fixing leguminous trees) will be favored. Preferably these will be trees which at the same time yield useful products. Trees which transpire large amounts may be used for drying poorly drained soils. Such trees may also have the good effect of slowing leaching by decreasing water percolation. From the standpoint of soil maintenance there is reason to grow a variety of plants. Different species make somewhat different demands upon the soil. As a result of the seasonal differences among them, those demands are made at different times. Furthermore, because of variations in size and stages of growth, the plants take nutrients from different depths in the soil.

Since competition is most intense for light and mineral nutrients, regulation of these factors will be a principal means of control. Shading is of further importance because where the soil is lateritic, long exposure to the sun may harden it to an almost brick-like consistency, rendering it unusable for a long time.

An important beginning in planning will be the description of periodicity in the whole useful flora and fauna of the area, and its relationship to seasonal changes in the physical environment and to human activities—in short, the preparation of a comprehensive tropical almanac. After a desirable assemblage of plants has been decided upon, selection will take into account the complex seasonal rhythms. Balances in the ecological system can be more easily shifted when critical instants in reproductive cycles are known; if the timing is judicious, desirable plants will have maximum competitive advantage. Bit by bit a new forest complex will be composed having an ideal harvest regime, so that one balanced cluster of useful species follows another as the year passes.

If a trial site were chosen (say a few square kilometers of but-slightly-disturbed forest) and the effects of selective processes such as those described above tested, using Indian workmen and knowledge, much would be learned—not only about man and nature in prehistoric tropical America but about rainforest resources for the future.

The table of additional native terms which appended will be useful to those exchanging information on the natural history of this area with its Guaymí and Bocatoreño inhabitants

Vernacular and Scientific Names for Plants

English	Spanish	Guaymí	Latin Binomial	Family
	aceituno	**menená**	*?*	
achiote	*anatto*	**kuró**	*Bixa orellana*	Bixaceae
aerial yam		**dru-gúagua**	*Dioscorea bulbifera?*	Dioscoreaceae
	ajito		*Cassipourea elliptica*	Rhizophoraceae
	almácigo		*Bursera simaruba*	Burseraceae
	almendro	**múru-be**	*Dipteryx panamensis*	Leguminosae
avocado (locally, "pear")	*pera*	**dugá**	*Persea americana*	Lauraceae
balsa	*balsa*	**krung**	*Ochroma pyramidale*	Bombacaceae
balsam apple	*balsamina*		*Momordica charantia*	Cucurbitaceae
banana	*guineo*	**ligimá**	*Musa sapientum*	Musaceae
	bateo	**adrurá**	*Carapa* sp.	Meliaceae
	bejuco negro		*Cordia spinescens*	Boraginaceae
	bejuco real	**tídra**	*?*	
	bribri	**bu-bulí**	*Inga minitula & I. punctata*	Leguminosae
cacao	*cacao*	**koá**	*Theobroma cacao*	Sterculiaceae
calabash	*jícara*	**síok**	*Crescentia cujete*	Bignoniaceae
candlewood	*caraña*	**nu**	*Trattinnickia aspera*	Burseraceae
	canjura	**kebo**	*Gnetum leyboldii*	Gnetaceae
caño-grass				
	carachero	**kevekría**	*Vismia macrophylla*	Guttiferae
	cerillo		*?*	
chayote	*chayote*		*Sechium edule*	Cucurbitaceae
	chica	**kungi**	*Arrabidaea chica*	Bignoniaceae
	chutra	**hudrángu**	*Protium panamensis*	Burseraceae
	cigarillo	**sule-gría**	*Jacaranda copaia*	Bignoniaceae
	cocito de mono	**kuarabá**	*Guarea multiflora*	Meliaceae
	cocoita		*?*	

English	Spanish	Guaymí	Latin Binomial	Family
coconut	*coco*	**kogó**	*Cocos nucifera*	Palmaceae
coco plum			*Chrysobalanus icaco*	Chrysobalanaceae
	conga	**huga**	*Oenocarpus panamanus?*	Palmaceae
	contra culebra		*Urospatha friedrichsthalia*	Araceae
cotton	*algodón*	**krundruá**	*Gossypium hirsutum*	Malvaceae
cow foot	*juánico*		*Piper auritum*	Piperaceae
	culantro	**druriá**	*Eryngium foetidum*	Umbelliferae
dasheen		**taw-doguá**	*Colocasia esculenta*	Araceae
dwarf palm		**nuru**	*Chamaedorea sp.*	Palmaceae
forest cacao	*cacao del monte*	**ko-kunge**	*Theobroma bernoullii*	Sterculiaceae
forest plum		**zobágria**	*Maripa panamensis*	Convolvulaceae
garden fern	*helecho*	**ka**	*Ctenitis sloanei*	Polypodiaceae
genipap	*jagua*		*Genipa americana*	Rubiaceae
gourd	*calabaza*	**murú**	*Lagenaria siceraria*	Cucurbitaceae
	granadilla		*Passiflora vitifolia*	Passifloraceae
ground palm		**dobogáw**	*Geonoma simplicifronds*	Palmaceae
	guágara	**huragá**	*Manicaria saccifera*	Palmaceae
	guamo del monte	**bunguágua**	*Inga* sp.	Leguminosae
	guarumo	**kurá**	*Cecropia* sps.	Moraceae
	guavo		*Inga edulis*	Leguminosae
guava	*guayava*		*Psidium guajava*	Myrtaceae
	guázumo		*Guazuma ulmifolia*	Sterculiaceae
	huesito		*Faramea* sp.	Rubiaceae
	jaboná		*Lacunaria panamensis*	Quiinaceae
jack-in-the-bush			*Calea prunifolia*	Compositae
jackass bitters			*Neurolaena lobata*	Compositae
	jira	**bugáda**	*Socratea durissima*	Palmaceae
	jirote	**tidí**	*Socratea?*	Palmaceae
job's tears			*Coix lachryma-jobi*	Graminae
johncrow wood	*yamerí*	**mi**	*Vochysia ferruginea*	Vochysiaceae

	kurutú	**zoborágria**	*Parkia* sp.	Leguminosae
lantana			*Lantana camera?*	Verbenaceae
	laurél		*Cordia alliodora*	Boraginaceae
maho	*majaguilla*		*Hibiscus tiliaceus*	Malvaceae
maize	*maiz*	**i**	*Zea mays*	Graminae
manatee grass			*Cymodocea manatorum?*	Graminae
mango	*mango*		*Mangifera indica*	Anacardiaceae
manioc	*yuca*	**u**	*Manihot utilissima*	Euphorbiaceae
margarita	*mala mujer*	**mingra**	*Wedelia trilobata*	Compositae
	mataratón		*Gliricidia sepium*	Leguminosae
	mato palo	**nuguánga**	*Oryctanthus cordifolius*	Loranthaceae
	mayo		?	
	membrillo	**tubáw**	*Gustavia superba*	Lecythidaceae
	membrillo del monte	**bui**	*Inga* sp.	Leguminosae
	membrillo silvestre		*Inga pezizifera*	Leguminosae
milk tree	*pera*	**mongrá**	*Conma macrocarpa*	Apocynaceae
	mocanguey		*Attalea allenii?*	Palmaceae
monkey apple	*fruta de mono*		*Posoqueria latifolia*	Rubiaceae
monkey comb	*corteza*	**muruvé**	*Apeiba membranacea*	Tiliaceae
monkey head		**siangóba**	*Licania platypus*	Chrysobalanaceae
monkey pot	*roble*	**za-odó**	*Couratari panamensis*	Lecythidaceae
	nance		*Byrsonima crassifolia*	Malpighiaceae
	nance de montaña		*Byrsonima* sp.	Malpighiaceae
	nancillo		*Citharexylum caudatum*	Verbenaceae
	ñampi	**drung**	*Dioscorea trifida*	Dioscoreaceae
	negrito	**dobináw**	*Ecclinusa guianensis*	Sapotaceae
	ojo de venado		*Mucuna mutisiana*	Leguminosae
	oreja de mula	**uranó**	*Bellucia axinanthera*	Melastomaceae
orey	*orí*	**ori-gria**	*Campnosperma panamensis*	Anacardiaceae
otó	*cocó*	**taw**	*Xanthosoma nigrum*	Araceae

English	Spanish	Guaymí	Latin Binomial	Family
	paja guinea		*Pennisetum purpureum*	Graminae
	palmito	**mídra**	*Welfia georgii*	Palmaceae
	palo espina		*Conostegia xalapensis*	Melastomaceae
panama-hat plant (wild broom)	*iraca (escobilla)*	**kimo**	*Carludovica palmata & C. drudei*	Cyclanthaceae
papaya	*papaya*		*Carica papaya*	Caricaceae
	pará		*Brachiaria mutica*	Graminae
	pataste	**odabá**	*Theobroma bicolor*	Sterculiaceae
	patatilla		*Melanthera aspera*	Compositae
peach palm	*pejibaye (piba)*	**dabá**	*Guilielma utilis*	Palmaceae
	pega-pega		*Desmodium canum*	Leguminosae
pigeon plum			*Hirtella latifolia*	Chrysobalanaceae
pineapple	*piña*		*Ananas comosus*	Bromeliaceae
plantain	*plátano*	**murú**	*Musa paradisiaca*	Musaceae
pokeweed	*calelu*	**sogá**	*Phytolacca rivinoides*	Phytolaccaceae
polewood	*jaja*	**surróna**	*Guatteria aeruginosa*	Annonaceae
provision tree		**unú**	*Pachira aquatica*	Bombacaceae
rancho palm		**ñuraná**	*Synechanthus warscewiczianus*	Palmaceae
raphia palm	*matumba (silico)*		*Raphia taedigera*	Palmaceae
	raska (raspa)		*Licania hypoleuca*	Chrysobalanaceae
reedwater tree			*Simara maxonii*	Rubiaceae
regrowth yam		**kebrú**	*Dioscorea standleyi?*	Dioscoreaceae
rose apple	*manzana*		*Eugenia malaccensis*	Myrtaceae
rubber tree	*caucho negro*	**kru-guádago**	*Castilla elastica*	Moraceae
sambergum	*cerillo*	**turáwba**	*Symphonia globulifera*	Guttiferae
sandbox tree	*ceibo*		*Hura crepitans*	Euphorbiaceae
	sándi	**noguáda**	*Pseudolmedia spuria*	Moraceae
	sangre		*Compsoneura sprucei*	Myristicaceae

	santa maria			
sapodilly	*níspero*	**toi-baw**	*Manilkara bidentata*	Sapotaceae
sarsaparilla (china root)	*zarza*		*Smilax panamensis?*	Smilacaceae
sea bean		**bóda**	*Entada monostachya*	Leguminosae
sea grape	*uva de playa*	**keglá**	*Coccoloba uvifera*	Polygonaceae
sensitive plant (shame weed)	*dormidera*		*Mimosa pudica*	Leguminosae
small-fruited passionflower	*granadilla*	**tibigué**	*Passiflora auriculata*	Passifloraceae
	sol-sol		*Alibertia garapatica*	Rubiaceae
soursop	*guanabana*		*Annona muricata*	Annonaceae
spider lily	*lirio de playa*		*Hymenocallis littoralis*	Amaryllidaceae
square-stemmed passionflower	*granadilla*	**kuguáta**	*Passiflora quadrangularis*	Passifloraceae
squash (pumpkin)	*auyama*	**be**	*Cucurbita moschata*	Cucurbitaceae
strangler fig		**muligría**	*Ficus* sp.	Moraceae
sugar cane	*caña*	**ibi-ya**	*Saccharum officinarum*	Graminae
swamp spiderlily	*lirio de agua*		*Crinum erubescens*	Amaryllidaceae
	tama-tama	**bui**	*Inga spectabilis*	Leguminosae
tapir palm		**modráwga**	*Geonoma sp.*	Palmaceae
tropical almond	*almendro*		*Terminalia catappa*	Combretaceae
turmeric		**sibrú**	*Curcuma longa*	Zingiberaceae
turtle grass			*Thalassia* sp.	Graminae
tropical cedar	*cedro*		*Cedrela odorata*	Meliaceae
vervain	*verbena*		*Stachytarpheta jamaicensis*	Verbenaceae
water hyacinth			*Eichhornia azurea*	Pontederiaceae
water vine		**buragé**	*Dolichocarpus major*	Dilleniaceae
wild banana	*bijao*	**krigo**	*Heliconia* sps.	Musaceae
wild cacao	*cacao cimarrón*	**hugé**	*Herrania purpurea*	Sterculiaceae

English	Spanish	Guaymí	Latin Binomial	Family
wild calabash			*Amphiteena latifolia*	Bignoniaceae
wild cane	*caña blanca (caña fleche)*	**iba-guadá**	*Gynerium sagittatum*	Graminae
wild lime			*Xylosma panamensis?*	Flacourtiaceae
wild membrillo			*Grias cauliflora*	Lecythidaceae
wild papaya			*Carica cauliflora*	Caricaceae
wild pineapple ("silk grass")	*pita*	**kigá**	*Aechmea magdalenae?*	Bromeliaceae
wild senna			*Cassia reticulata*	Leguminosae
wild soursop	*guanabana cimarrón*	**surróng**	*Annona glabra*	Annonaceae
wild sweet potato	*batata cimarrón*		*Ipomea acuminata?*	Convolvulaceae
wild tama-tama	*guavo del monte*	**buí**	*Inga goldmanii*	Leguminosae
yellow mombin (hog plum)	*jobo*	**hogó**	*Spondias mombin*	Anacardiaceae
	zacote		*Echinochloa polystacha*	Graminae

Vernacular and Scientific Names for Animals

English	Spanish	Guaymí	Latin Binomial
Mollusks			
	chililé	**chelé**	*Neritina clenchi*
fighting stromb (locally, "conch")	*caracol*	**drrú**	*Strombus pugilis*
Insects			
firefly	*cucullo*	**tandú**	
honeybee (stingless native species)	*abeja*	**mungána**	*Trigona frontalis*
wax insect		**kurrón**	*Llaveia axin*
Other Invertebrates			
spiny lobster	*langosta*		*Panulirus argus*
sea urchin		**negen-tukuá**	
white land crab		**ludi**	*Cardisoma guanhumi*
Fish			
barracuda			*Sphyraena*
califéva	*lebranche*	**sadu**	*Mugil cephalus*
	boca chica	**ua-krí**	*Prochilodus?*
eel	*anguila*	**durú**	
grouper			*Epinephelus?*
kingfish			
snooker	*robalo*	**dugai**	*Centropomus?*
tarpon	*sabalo*		*Tarpon* sp.
	tití	**dubú**	*Sicydium* sp.

English	Spanish	Guaymí	Latin Binomial
Turtles			
freshwater turtle	*jicotea*	**será**	
green turtle	*tortuga verde*	**ñiel-iéro**	*Chelonia mydas*
hawksbill (carey)	*tortuga mulato*	**tu-bú**	*Eretmochelys imbricata*
loggerhead	*tortuga cahuama*	**tubú-daguá**	*Caretta caretta*
trunk or leather-back ("trunky")	*canál*	**didi-yó**	*Dermochelys coriacea*
Lizards			
iguana	*iguana*	**du**	
"jesus" lizard	*moracho*	**hidrási**	*Basilicus galeritus*
Snakes			
fer-de-lance		**krundíbi**	*Bothrops atrox*
bushmaster		**íja**	*Lachaesis muta?*
boa	*boa*	**ñurdibi**	
black snake		**hurin-dibi**	
Birds			
ani	*tico*	**klóa**	*Crotophaga*
brown booby			*Sula leucogaster*
cattle egret			*Bubulcus ibis*
chachalaca	*faisán*	**ura-ri**	*Ortalis cinereiceps*
chestnut-mandibled toucan		**kiala**	*Ramphastos swainsonii*
chicken (domesticated)	*gallina*	**quí**	
collared aricari		**bisilí**	*Pteroglossus torquatus*
common tody flycatcher			*Todirostrum cinereum*

crimson-fronted parakeet			*Aratinga finschi*
curassow	*pavón*	**iri-uí**	*Crax rubra*
gray-necked woodrail	*cocoleca*	**kon-seré**	*Aramides cajanea*
great-tailed grackle			*Cassidix mexicanus*
great tinamou	*perdice de montaña*	**moso-loró**	*Tinamus major*
guan	*pava*	**kueli**	*Penelope purpurascens*
keel-billed toucan		**kueré**	*Ramphastos sulfuratus*
kingfisher (ringed)	*martín*	**dúa**	*Ceryle torquata*
little tinamou	*perdice de rastrojo*	**suéra**	*Crypturellas soui*
long-tailed tyrant			*Colonia colonus*
muscovy duck		**ma-dó**	*Cairina moschata*
pelican (brown)		**dukú**	*Pelecanus occidentalis*
scaled pigeon	*torcaza*	**udui-krí**	*Columba speciosa*
short-billed pigeon	*guarumero*		*Columba nigrirostris*
social flycatcher			*Myiozetetes similis*
sunbittern		**kerulí**	*Eurypyga helias*
variable (black) seedeater	*huachito*	**ye-lí**	*Sporophila aurita*
vulture (black) "john crow"		**chan**	*Coragyps atratus*
white-collared seedeater			*Sporophila torqueola*
white-throated crake		**buragí**	*Laterallus albigularis*
Mammals			
agouti	*ñeque*	**muría**	*Dasyprocta punctata*
anteater, giant		**mé**	*Myrmecophaga*
lesser (tamandua)		**me-solí**	*Tamandua*

English	Spanish	Guaymí	Latin Binomial
armadillo			
("ground hog")		**nu-sí**	*Dasypus novemcinctus*
cow		**nibí**	
deer brocket	*venao colorado*	**burra**	*Mazama americana*
white-tailed	*venao de rama*	**burra-nué**	*Odocoileus chiriquensis*
dog		**nu-grro**	
jaguar	*tigre*	**kurá**	
manatee			*Trichechus*
monkey, spider		**chowá**	*Ateles*
capuchin		**drróa**	*Cebus capucinus*
howler		**hurrí**	*Alouatta*
ocelot		**kura-chi**	*Felis pardalis*
opossum, common		**kodá**	*Didelphis marsupialis*
mouse		**kodaló**	*Marmosa*
otter ("water dog")	*gato de agua*	**nú**	*Lutra*
paca	*conejo*	**ñuá**	*Cuniculus paca*
peccary collared	*zahino*	**mudi-kiári**	*Pecari angulatus*
white lipped	*manado*	**mudi-krí**	*Tayassu pecari*
puma	*león*	**kura-tai**	*Felis concolor*
rabbit	*muleto*	**mu-ló**	*Sylvilagus*
rat, cotton			*Sigmodon*
rice			*Oryzomys*
spined			
("porcupine")	*macangue*	**ñio-tugili**	*Hoplomys*
skunk		**ku-gali**	*Conepatus?*
sloth, two-toed		**ku-dolí**	
squirrel	*ardita*	**kon dáw**	*Sciurus*
tapir			
("mountain cow")	*danta*	**mu lá**	*Tapirus bairdii*

LITERATURE CITED

Allen, Paul H. 1956. *The Rainforests of Golfo Dulce.* University of Florida Press, Gainesville.

Alphonse, E.S. 1956. Guaymí Grammar and Dictionary. *Smithsonian Institution, Bureau of of American Ethnology,* Bulletin 162, Washington, D.C.

Bartlett, H.H. 1936. A Method of Procedure for Field Work in Tropical American Phytogeo-geography Based Upon a Botanical Reconnaissance in Parts of British Honduras and the Petén Forest of Guatemala. *Botany of the Maya Area: Miscellaneous Papers,* Carnegie Institute of Washington Publication, No. 461, Washington, D.C.

Bennett, C.F. 1968. The Influence of Contemporary Man on the Zoogeography of the Panama Land Bridge, Panama. *Ibero-Americana,* Vol. 51, University of California Press, Berkeley and Los Angeles.

Contraloría General de la República. 1950. *Estadística panameña demografía, República de Panamá.* Panama City.

————. 1962. Lugares poblados de la República. *Censos Nacionales de* 1960, Vol. I.

Cook, O.F. 1909. Vegetation Affected by Agriculture in Central America. *Bureau of Plant Industry,* Bul. 145, Washington, D.C.

————. 1935. The Maya Breadnut in Southern Florida. *Science,* Vol. 82, pp. 615-616.

Cornwaite, H.G. 1919. Panama Rainfall. *Monthly Weather Review,* Vol. 17, Washington, D.C.

Croat, T.B. 1969. Seasonal Flowering Behavior in Central Panama. *Annals of the Missouri Botanical Garden,* Vol. 56, No. 3, pp. 259-307.

————. 1978. *Flora of Barro Colorado Island.* Stanford University Press.

Duke, J.A. 1969. On Tropical Tree Seedlings. *Annals of the Missouri Botanical Garden,* Vol. 56, No. 2.

Eeckhout, L.E. 1953. L'exploitation forestiere au Congo Belge. *Ministére des Colonies,* Brussels.

Eisenmann, E. 1957. Notes on Birds of the Province of Bocas del Toro, Panama. *Condor,* Vol. 59, pp. 247-262.

Gabb, W.M. 1875. On the Indian Tribes and Languages of Costa Rica. *Proceedings of the American Philosophical Society,* Vol. 14, Philadelphia.

Gentry, P. 1973. Flora of Panama (Bignoniaceae). *Annals of the Missouri Botanical Garden,* Vol. 60.

Goldman, E.A. 1920. Mammals of Panama. *Smithsonian Miscellaneous Collections,* Vol. 69, No. 5, Washington, D.C.

Gordon, B.L. 1957A. Human Geography and Ecology in the Sinú Country of Colombia. *Ibero-Americana,* Vol. 39, University of California Press, Berkeley and Los Angeles.

————. 1957B. A Domesticated Wax-Producing, Scale Insect Kept by the Guaymí Indians of Panamá. *Ethnos,* Vol. 22, Nos. 1-2, pp. 36-49, Stockholm.

————. 1961. *Notes on the Chiriquí Lagoon District and Adjacent Regions of Panamá,* ONR Contract 222 (ii) NR338 067.

————. 1962. Notes on Shell Mounds Near the Caribbean Coast of Western Panamá. *Panama Archaeologist,* Vol. 5, Panama City.

————. 1969. *Anthropogeography and Rainforest Ecology in Bocas del Toro Province, Panamá,* University of California, Dept. of Geog., Berkeley, 99 pp.

————. 1979. Monterey Bay Area: Natural History and Cultural Imprints, 2nd edition, The Boxwood Press, Pacific Grove, California.

Haines, B. 1975. Impact of Leaf-cutting Ants on Vegetation Development at Barro Colorado Island. *Tropical Ecological Systems,* (F.B. Golley and E. Medina, eds.), Springer-Verlag, N.Y. and Berlin.

Howe, H.F. 1977. Bird Activity and Seed Dispersal of a Tropical Wet Forest Tree. *Ecology,* Vol. 58, pp. 539-550.

Izikowitz, K.G. 1935. *Musical and Other Sound Instruments of the South American Indians.* Goteborg.

Janzen, D.H. 1970. Herbivores and the Number of Tree Species in Tropical Forests. *The American Naturalist,* Vol. 104, pp. 501-528.

Johnson, F. 1959. The Caribbean Lowland Tribes. The Talamanca Division. *Handbook of South American Indians,* Vol. 4, Washington, D.C.

Kenoyer, L.A. 1929. General and Successional Ecology of the Lower Tropical Rainforest at Barro Colorado Island, Panama. *Ecology,* Vol. 10, Brooklyn and New York.

Leck, C.F. 1970. Comments on the Seasonality of Fruiting in the Neotropics. *The American Naturalist,* Vol. 104, pp. 583-584.

Léon Fernández. 1881-1907. *Colección de Documentos para la Historia de Costa Rica,* 10 tomos, San José, Paris, Barcelona.

Levi-Strauss, C. 1950. The Use of Wild Plants in Tropical South America, *Handbook of South American Indians,* (ed. J.H. Steward). Smithsonian Institution, Bureau of American Ethnology, Bull. 143, Vol. 6, Washington, D.C.

Lothrop, S.K. 1937. Coclé. An Archaeological Study of Central Panama. *Memoirs of the Peabody Museum of Archaeology and Ethnology, Harvard University,* Vol. VII, Cambridge, Massachusetts.

————. 1942. The Sigua: Southwest Aztec Outpost. *Proceedings of the Eighth American Scientific Congress,* Vol. 2, pp. 109-116, Washington, D.C.

————. 1950. Archaeology of Southern Veraguas, Panama. (With Appendices by W.C. Root, Eleanor B. Adams, and Doris Stone). *Memoirs of the Peabody Museum of Archaeology and Ethnology, Harvard University,* Vol. IX, No. 3, Cambridge, Massachusetts.

Lumholtz, K.S. 1920. *Unknown Mexico.* New York.

Lundell, C.L. 1933. The Agriculture of the Maya. *Southwest Review,* Vol. 10, pp. 65-77, Dallas.

Morison, S.E. 1942. *Admiral of the Ocean Sea.* Little, Brown and Company, Boston.

Morley, S.C. 1947. *The Ancient Maya.* Stanford University, Palo Alto.

Morris, P.A. 1973. *A Field Guide to Shells of the Atlantic and Gulf Coasts and the West Indies.* Houghton Mifflin Company, Boston.

Oppenheimer, J.R. and G.E. Lang. 1969. Cebus Monkey: Effect on Branching of *Gustavia* Trees. *Science,* Vol. 165, pp. 187-188.

Oviedo y Valdés, G.F. de. 1851-1855. *Historia general y natural de las Indias, islas y tierra firme del mar océano.* Madrid.

Ower, L.H. 1928. *The Geology of British Honduras.* Belize.

Parsons, J.J. 1954. English Speaking Settlement in the Western Caribbean. *Yearbook of the Association of Pacific Coast Geographers,* Vol. 16, pp. 3-16.

————. 1972. Spread of African Pasture Grasses to the American Tropics. *Journal of Range Management,* Vol. 25, pp. 12-17.

————. 1976. Forest to Pasture: Development or Destruction? *Revista de Biología Tropical,* Vol. 24 (Supl. 1), pp. 121-138.

Pinart, A.L. 1885. *Chiriquí: Bocas del Toro-Valle Miranda.* Paris.

Pittier de Fabrega, H. 1893. "Ensayo lexicográfico sobre la Lengua de Térraba." *Anales del Instituto Fisico-Geográfico y del Museo Nacional de Costa Rica,* Vol. 4, pp. 71-100, San José de Costa Rica.

————. 1903. "Die Tírub: Terribes oder Térrabas, ein im Aussterben begriffener Stamm in Costa Rica." *Zeitschrift für Ethnologie,* Vol. 35, Berlin.

————. 1908. *Ensayo sobre las Plantas usuales de Costa Rica.* Washington, D.C.

————. 1918. "Our Present Knowledge of the Forest Formations of Panama." *Journal of Forestry,* Vol. 16, Washington, D.C.

Portig, W.H. 1965. "Central American Rainfall." *Geographical Review,* Vol. 55, pp. 68-90.

Pulleston, D.E. 1971. "An Ecological Approach to the Origins of Maya Civilization." *Archaeology,* Vol. 24, pp. 330-337.

Rebel, T.P. 1974. *Sea Turtles and the Turtle Industry of the West Indies, Florida, and the Gulf of Mexico.* University of Miami Press, Coral Gables, Florida.

Ridgely, R.S. 1976. *A Guide to the Birds of Panama.* Princeton University Press, Princeton, N.J.

Salcedo, J. 1908. *Relaciones históricas y geográficas de América Central.* Madrid.

Sapir, O.L. de and A.J. Ranere. 1971. "Tropical Forests of Western Panama." *Archaeology,* Vol. 24, pp. 346-355.

Sapper, K. 1902. "Die Geographische Bedeutung der Mittelamerikanischen Vulkane." *Zeitschrift der Gesellschaft für Erdkunde zu Berlin,* Berlin.

Sauer, C.O. 1950. "Cultivated Plants of South America." *Handbook of South American Indians,* Smithsonian Institution, Bureau of American Ethnology, Bull. 143, Vol. 6, Washington, D.C.

————. 1952. *Agricultural Origins and Dispersals.* The American Geographical Society, New York.

————. 1966. *The Early Spanish Main.* University of California Press, Berkeley and Los Angeles.

Schimper, A.F.W. 1903. *Plant Geography Upon a Physiological Basis.* Oxford.
Schneider, F. 1939. "Ein Vergleich von Urwald und Monokultur in Bezug auf ihre Gefahrdung durch phytophage Insecten, auf Grund einiger Beobachtungen an der Ostküste von Sumatra." *Schweiz, Zeitschr. Forstw.*, 90:41-55, 82-89.
Seeman, B. 1854. *The Botany of the Voyage of the HMS Herald, 1945-1851.* Reeve, London.
Seibert, R.J. 1940. "The Bignoniaceae of the Maya Area." *Botany of the Maya Area: Miscellaneous Papers,* Carnegie Institute of Washington,Washington, D.C.
Seler, E. 1908. "Puerto de San Gerónimo, Coaza, und das Valle de Guaymí." *Gesammelte Abhandlungen zur Amerikanischen Sprach-und Alterthumskunde,* Vol. 3, Berlin.
Skutch, A.F. 1945. "The Most Hospitable Tree." *Scientific Monthly,* January, pp. 5-17.
————. 1946. "Palm Forests." *Nature,* Vol. 39, pp. 135-135.
————. 1949. "The Panama Hat Plant." *Nature,* Vol. 42, pp. 173-175.
————. 1950. "The Nesting Seasons of Central American Birds in Relation to Climate and Food Supply." *The Ibis,* Vol. 92, pp. 185-221.
————. 1963. "Life History of the Little Tinamou." *Condor,* Vol. 65, pp. 224-231.
Smythe, N. 1970. "Relationship Between Fruiting Seasons and Seed Dispersal in a Neotropical Forest." *American Naturalist,* Vol. 104, pp. 25-35.
Soderstrom, J. 1937. "Some Notes on the Poi and Other Preserved Vegetation in the Pacific." *Ethnos,* Vol. 1, No. 3, pp. 235-242, Stockholm.
Spinden, H.J. 1928. "Population of Ancient America." *The Geographical Review,* Vol. 18, pp. 641-660, New York.
Standley, P.C. 1928. "Flora of the Panama Canal Zone." *Contributions of the United States National Herbarium,* Vol. 27, Washington, D.C.
————. 1937. "Flora of Costa Rica." *Botanical Series, Field Museum of Natural History,* Vol. 18, Parts I-II, Chicago.
Standley, R.E. and R.W. Schery. 1950. "Flora of Panama (Rosaceae)." *Annals of the Missouri Botanical Garden.*
————. 1958. "Flora of Panama (Passifloraceae)." *Annals of the Missouri Botanical Garden.*
Stark, N.M. 1971. "Mycorrhizae and Nutrient Cycling in the Tropics." *Mycorrhizae* (E. Hacskaylo, ed.), U.S. Govt. Printing Office, Washington, D.C.
Stewart, T.D. 1942. "Persistence of the African Type of Tooth Pointing in Panama." *American Anthropologist,* n.s., Vol. 44, pp. 328-330, Menasha, Wisconsin.
Stirling, M.W. 1953. "Hunting Prehistory in Panama Jungles." *National Geographic Magazine,* Vol. 104, No. 2, pp. 271-290, Washington, D.C.
Stone, D.Z. 1949. "The Boruca of Costa Rica." *Papers of the Peabody Museum of American Archaeology and Ethnology, Harvard University,* Vol. 26, No. 2, Cambridge, Massachusetts.
————. 1962. "The Talamancan Tribes of Costa Rica." *Papers of the Peabody Museum of American Archaeology and Ethnology, Harvard University,* Vol. 43, No. 2, Cambridge Massachusetts.
Terborgh, J. 1975. "Faunal Equilibria and the Design of Wildlife Preserves." *Tropical Ecological Systems* (F.B. Golley and E. Medina, eds.), Springer-Verlag, N.Y. and Berlin.
Terry, R.A. 1956. "A Geological Reconnaissance of Panama." *Occasional Papers of the California Academy of Science,* No. 23, San Francisco.
Tessmann, G. 1930. *Die Indianer Nordost-Peru.* Hamburg.
Thiel, B.A. 1892. "Itinerarios de los Misioneros Franciscanos en Talamanca." *Anales del Instituto Fisico-Geográfico y del Museo Nacional de Costa Rica,* Vol. 3, San José.
Vezga, F. 1936. "Botánica Indígena." *Biblioteca Aldeana de Colombia, Bogotá,* Vol. 47.
Wassen, S.H. 1951. "Some Remarks on the Divisions of the Guaymí Indians." *Indian Tribes of Aboriginal America* (Sol Tax, ed.) Chicago.
Wetmore, A. "The Birds of Isla Escudo de Veraguas, Panama." *Smithsonian Misc. Collections,* Vol. 139, No. 2, pp. 1-27.
————. 1972. "The Birds of the Republic of Panama." *Smithsonian Miscellaneous Collections,* Vol. 150, Smithsonian Institution Press.
Wunderlin, R.P. 1978. "Cucurbitacea" in *Flora of Panama* by Robert E. Woodson, Jr. and Robert W. Schery and Collaborators, *Annals of the Missouri Botanical Garden,* Vol. 65, No. 1.
Young, P.D. 1971. "Ngawbe. Tradition and Change Among the Western Guaymí of Panama." *Illinois Studies in Anthropology,* No. 7, University of Illinois Press, Urbana.

INDEX